This short, scholarly, insigh
aids readers to interact with t
25-37. Davis joins hands with the sacred songwriter in
beckoning us to employ our grittiest grief, formidable
fears, principal praises and staunchest certainties as we
pour out our hearts into the bosom of God. This work
is ideal for preachers and parishioners in study, but even
more, devotionally. And if you are trudging arduously
before the oppressive presence of evil and darkness, you
will find this book a true friend!

Michael W. Philliber
Senior Pastor, Heritage Presbyterian Church (PCA),
Oklahoma City, Oklahoma

Few Bible teachers have influenced me more than Dale
Ralph Davis. His preaching and writing on the psalms
are my favorites. In this work of exposition, Davis again
shows how unchanging God's Word is, and how sufficient
He is to meet us in whatever trial we face. Davis has a gift
for bringing the Word to bear in clear and crisp ways.
This book does just that—and it's another gift to God's
people from Dr. Davis.

Courtney Reissig
Author, *Teach Me to Feel: Worshiping Through the Psalms in Every
Season of Life*

Read *In the Presence of My Enemies* and you will find
yourself richly blessed by its wonderfully inspirational and
thoroughly biblical content. Your mind will be stimulated,
your heart warmed, your faith excited and strengthened
and your soul spiritually uplifted and enriched. You will

have cause to feel indebted to Dale Ralph Davis for what he offers in this timely book of studies in selected psalms. I am quite persuaded that Christians of all ages and levels of spiritual maturity and experience, including those who have been called of God to be preachers of His Word, will not regret the giving of their time to the careful reading of this excellent book. It is Ralph Davis at his best. Brilliant exposition punctuated by apt historical illustrations, pertinent quotations, home spun stories, personal honesty and delicious use of language.

David Carmichael
Minister, Abbeygreen Church, Lesmahagow, Scotland
Chairman, Scottish Reformed Conference

I couldn't be more pleased that Dr. Davis has added to his expositions on the Psalms. His writing contains the unique and delightful combination of a Hebrew scholar's knowledge and a kind grandfather's penchant for storytelling wrapped up in the wisdom of an experienced pastor. The treasure of this book is the way Dr. Davis skillfully walks his readers through the ancient words and literary styles of these Psalms into a grander view of the covenant-keeping God and a fuller understanding of His care for His people.

Emily Woodard
Director of Women's Ministry, First Presbyterian Church,
Columbia, South Carolina

Conflict and enemies: one doesn't get very far in life and ministry without being introduced to both of them and the wounds and scars they bequeath. So this accessible but profound study of the Psalms has warmed my heart and made me thankful again for the greater gift of Christ our King. There is gold on every page and comfort in each chapter. Once again we are all in Dale Ralph Davis' debt for his scholarship presented with humility and his ministry fulfilled so faithfully.

David Gibson
Minister, Trinity Church Aberdeen, Scotland

Ralph Davis loves baseball. Well, this exposition of Psalms 25-37 is not only a home run, but a grand slam home run. Christians love to read the Old Testament Psalms, but we often struggle to grasp the flow and meaning of the text. Ralph pulls back the veil and helps us to see the height, depth, length and breadth of the love of Yahweh for His people in all ages of the church. This exposition will provide fuel for the souls of those who read it.

David Jussely
Adjunct Professor, Reformed Theological Seminary, Jackson, Mississippi
Associate Pastor, First Presbyterian Church, Hattiesburg, Mississippi

IN THE PRESENCE OF MY ENEMIES

Psalms 25-37

Dale Ralph Davis

CHRISTIAN
FOCUS

Copyright © Dale Ralph Davis 2020

paperback ISBN 978-1-5271-0479-2
epub ISBN 978-1-5271-0541-6
Mobi ISBN 978-1-5271-0542-3

10 9 8 7 6 5 4 3 2 1

Printed in 2020
by
Christian Focus Publications Ltd.,
Geanies House, Fearn, Ross-shire,
IV20 1TW, Scotland, Great Britain
www.christianfocus.com

Cover design by Daniel Van Straaten
Printed in the USA

Contents

Abbreviations

ABD	*Anchor Bible Dictionary*
CSB	Christian Standard Bible
DCH	*Dictionary of Classical Hebrew*
EBC	*The Expositor's Bible Commentary*
ESV	English Standard Version
K-B	Koehler and Baumgartner, *Hebrew and Aramaic Lexicon*
NASB	New American Standard Bible
NIDOTTE	*New International Dictionary of Old Testament Theology & Exegesis*
NIV	New International Version
NJB	New Jerusalem Bible
NJPS	Tanakh: A New Translation of the Holy Scriptures according to the Traditional Hebrew Text (1985)
NKJV	New King James Version
NLT	New Living Translation
NRSV	New Revised Standard Version
NT	New Testament
OT	Old Testament
RSV	Revised Standard Version
TCNT	Twentieth Century New Testament
TEV	Today's English Version
TWOT	*Theological Wordbook of the Old Testament*

Preface

'I'm living in the Psalms,' I believe my friend told me. He was going through a 'deep waters' time and the Psalms were proving to be where he met the Lord who both understood and undergirded him. Scads of saints would say the same. But if the Psalms are helpful, they are also hard. At least I find them so, when trying to write expositions of them. It's slow, plodding, sweaty work; but here, at any rate, are a dozen or so more.

I've tried to keep the style informal, though I have included a few references or notes in these expositions. The translations are my own, and I continue to use 'Yahweh' for the personal, covenant name of God instead of the traditional 'the LORD' (see *The Way of the Righteous in the Muck of Life*, p.8, for an explanation). If God has revealed His personal name to us, it seems a shame not to use His 'first name' in texts as personal and intense as the Psalms.

I am aware that the title comes from Psalm 23:5 and not from any of the Psalms treated here. But most of them deal with conflicts and enemies and so I didn't think David would mind my stealing the rubric from Psalm 23. And I'd like to send out this study in honor of relatively recent friends who seem like old friends, Calvin and Lisa Todd. Calvin and I overlapped for about five years while serving on the staff of First Presbyterian, Columbia, South Carolina, and found that we shared the same 'prejudices' about ministry! And even though I don't hunt or fish, he still accepted me as his friend.

Psalm 25

Of David.

(1) To you, O Yahweh, I lift up my soul.

(2) My God, I have trusted in you;
let me not be put to shame;
don't let my enemies gloat over me.

(3) Indeed, all who wait for you will never be put to shame;
those who are treacherous for no reason will be put to shame.

(4) Make me to know your ways, Yahweh,
teach me your paths.

(5) Lead me in your faithfulness and teach me,
for you are the God of my salvation;
you are the one I wait for all day long.

(6) Remember your compassions, Yahweh,
and your acts of grace,
for they are from everlasting.

(7) Do not remember the sins of my youth or my rebellions;
in line with your unfailing love you must remember me
on account of your goodness, Yahweh.

(8) Yahweh is good and upright;
therefore he teaches sinners in the way (to go).

(9)   He will lead the humble in justice,
       and he will teach the humble his way.

(10) All the paths of Yahweh are unfailing love and faithfulness
       to those who keep his covenant and his testimonies.

(11) On account of your name, Yahweh,
       you must pardon my guilt, for it is great.

(12) Who is the man who fears Yahweh?
       He will instruct him in the way he should choose.

(13) His soul will remain in goodness
       and his seed will possess the land.

(14) The closeness of Yahweh is for those fearing him,
       and his covenant he makes known to them.

(15) My eyes are continually toward Yahweh,
       for **he** will bring out my feet from the net.

(16) Turn to me and show grace to me,
       for I am alone and afflicted.

(17) They have enlarged the troubles of my heart
       – bring me out of my difficulties.

(18) Look on my affliction and my trouble
       – and forgive all my sins.

(19) Look on my enemies, for they have multiplied,
       and they hate me with vicious hatred.

(20) Watch over my soul and deliver me;
       don't let me be ashamed,
       for I have taken refuge in you.

(21) Whole-heartedness and uprightness will preserve me,
       for I have waited for you.

(22) Redeem Israel, O God,
       from all his troubles.

Alphabetting Toward Deliverance

1

Once every month our church puts on a lunch for university students after the second worship service, and my wife usually volunteers to provide a dessert. However, it is a highly regimented dessert. One cannot freewheel. There may be six or eight people providing desserts. The dessert is specified. Foil pans are provided. There is a standard recipe to be followed. Let's say it is banana pudding. The recipe will specify how many bananas are to be sliced, what kind and how much vanilla pudding mix is to be used, how thick the layer of 'Cool Whip' on the top is to be, and so on. All this 'controls' the process and all contributions are pretty much the same. All dessert-makers have to work within that structure.

That's the way it is with Psalm 25. It follows an acrostic structure, in which each verse begins with the subsequent letter of the Hebrew alphabet (for the most part). Since the psalm must adhere to this alphabetical pattern there can be certain consequences. For instance, it may be harder to trace connected lines of thought in the psalm. Not a big deal, but those of us with a western kind of thought process like to carve things up in manageable, coherent chunks and that can be harder to do when a writer is focusing on telling about something following an A-to-Z, item-by-item, pattern. However, as long as we don't try to be too rigid, I think we can see certain *dominant emphases* as we walk through the psalm.

The first of these we may call **petitions** (vv. 1-7). There are several matters David prays about here and the first is for *the relief of God's deliverance* (vv. 1-3). His prayer here strikes notes of assurance in verses 1 and 3 with his petition sandwiched in between in verse 2. That plea is: 'Let me not be put to shame; don't let my enemies gloat over me' (v. 2b). Yet note with his plea the sure confidence, especially in verse 3: 'Indeed, all who wait for you will never be put to shame; those who are treacherous for no reason will be put to shame.' Such a resounding, Apostles'-Creed-type certainty in verse 3, and yet in verse 2 the very same matter pressed in urgent prayer. All of which is not contradictory but rather instructive. How are we to express our faith in Yahweh's vindication (v. 3) except in our prayer in instances of such particular need (v. 2)? Indeed, are not most of our prayers a mix of assurance (vv. 1, 3) and anxiety (v. 2), of trust and trouble?

His second petition is for *the enjoyment of God's ways* (vv. 4-5): 'Make me to know your ways, Yahweh, teach me your paths.' And then, 'Lead me in your faithfulness.' What are we to make of these 'ways' and 'paths'? We usually think of them, I suppose, as the ways of God's commandments, the ways He requires of us. And sometimes that is clearly the sense (e.g., Exod. 32:8; Ps. 119:32, 33). But the more I ponder this text the more I lean to J. A. Alexander's position that here the 'ways' and 'paths' are not referring to the ways God commands but to the ways He *operates*, not to the ways of precepts but of *providence*, not what He demands but how He deals with His people.[1] Verse 5a seems to support this, since the traditional 'lead me in your truth' is better translated 'in your faithfulness'. Moreover, verse 10 seems to carry the same sense: 'All the paths of Yahweh are unfailing love and faithfulness to those who keep his covenant and testimonies.' So he seems to be praying that Yahweh will teach him how He is working in his case (v. 4) and to let him experience His faithfulness (v. 5) as he goes on. Isn't this what so thrills a Christian believer? He or she can look back and sometimes trace those 'ways' of the saving God. Ways and paths that sometimes seemed twisted, looking as if they operated by hook or by crook, and yet we found that disappointments led to deliverances, frustrations to escapes from temptations, and difficulties strangely prevented disaster. And when the Lord gives us a glimpse of those ways, we know why we long for Him all day long (v. 5b).

David's third petition seeks *the warmth of God's compassions* (vv. 6-7). He uses the verb 'remember' (*zākar*) three times, two positively and one in between these two negatively:

---

1   J. A. Alexander, *The Psalms Translated and Explained* (1864; reprint ed., Grand Rapids: Zondervan, n.d.), 114-15.

> Remember your compassions ... acts of grace ...
>
> Do not remember the sins of my youth or my rebellions ...
>
> In line with your unfailing love you must remember me ...

Yahweh's compassions and acts of grace (lit., 'your *ḥeseds*') are 'from everlasting'. So verse 6 speaks of a whole, ongoing history of divine kindness. The phrase 'from everlasting' reminds us that Yahweh has always been this way! Cynical students at a small college sometimes observe that on days when potential new students visit the campus the food service really puts out an impressive meal or two. But after the visitors are gone it all reverts to much poorer fare. But Yahweh is not like that – compassions and grace are His always-style of operating. Then David asks for a particular instance of Yahweh's kindness: 'do not remember the sins of my youth and my rebellions' (v. 7a). David *can* remember them; that's why he asks Yahweh not to do so. How the 'sins of (our) youth' can come parading before us! And they may not have been racily godless ones. Simply that I manipulated people, that sometimes I *desired* to hurt them, that I had little conscious gratitude for all I had received, that I was, as sadly I have always been, wrapped up in an idolatry of self. How marvelous then a non-remembering God!

I hesitate a bit to pass on an anecdote that once appeared in *Leadership* magazine, because it may appear to be too mystical. There was a woman in a town in the Philippines who was said to have intimate converse with the Lord.

A local priest decided to test her and told her that next time she had such a 'conference' to ask Him what sin her priest had committed while he was in seminary. Some time later he saw the woman and asked, 'Did you speak with Him?' 'Yes.' 'What did He say?' 'He said, "I don't remember."' The amnesia of divine forgiveness is more than we can take in.

These are David's petitions – for deliverance, for understanding, for pardon.

Secondly, David's prayer focuses primarily on **provisions** (vv. 8-14). Here most of the prayer consists of declarations about Yahweh – perhaps we would do well to speak more in this way in our own prayers. The first area of provision has to do with *direction and forgiveness* (vv. 8-11).

In verses 8-9, 'the way' and 'his way' refer to the direction His people are to take in agreement with Yahweh's will. He even 'teaches sinners in the way' (v. 8b). No one then should claim he is too alienated from the Lord, beyond help and hope, for Yahweh will show him the way of recovery. And He leads and teaches 'the humble' (v. 9), a word that refers to Yahweh's own battered and beaten down people (Motyer translates it as 'downtrodden'). They may be clobbered and detested in the world, but they are objects of Yahweh's directing care. All of which means that 'all the paths of Yahweh are unfailing love and faithfulness' (v. 10a). Here we are back to thinking of the ways Yahweh operates toward His people (vv. 4-5). Which leads into a petition amid all these declarations:

> On account of your name, Yahweh,
> you must pardon my guilt,
> for it is great (v. 11).

He is allowing the concern of verse 7 to re-surface. He bases his petition on Yahweh's *declared character* – 'on account of your name.' That is, because of what you have said yourself to be, or, as verse 10 has just said, because all your paths are 'unfailing love and faithfulness', because you are that way, because that is your character and disposition, because that is what you are like, you must pardon. But then he also appeals for pardon on the basis of his *massive need*: 'pardon my guilt, for it is great.'[2] Jonathan Edwards once preached a sermon on this text[3] and noted the 'surprising' logic involved: David made no plea about doing so much good to counter-balance his iniquity, nor did he claim his iniquity was really relatively small; rather he pled the sheer immensity of his need as the claim for forgiveness. As CSB has it: 'forgive my iniquity, for it is immense.'

Perhaps we don't 'feel' the immensity of our guilt; that may be because we tend to limit our scope to sins of 'commission' and 'omission'. But a little thought can reveal far more of our corruption and guilt than we want to see. Simply consider your reactions in the common run of life. Several days ago I was frustrated by my 'weed-whacker',

---

2   I am aware that NIV and NJPS translate the closing clause, 'though it is great,' that is, in a 'concessive' sense rather than a causal one. But the particle *kî* more likely retains the causal sense here – 'for/because it is great.'

3   See *The Works of Jonathan Edwards*, 2 vols. (1834; reprint ed., Peabody, MA: Hendrickson, 1998), 2:110-11.

that nefarious instrument for trimming and edging the yard. I had just purchased this new one several weeks before and was in the process of performing an 'operation' on it – I wanted to remove the cutting line mechanism that came with the 'whacker' and replace it with an alternate mechanism in which replacing the cutting line would be much easier. But there were problems. I couldn't get the original cutting head off of the weed-whacker and in trying to do so I basically mangled the thing. Now the whole weed-whacker was essentially unredeemable and useless and, of course, frustration mounted. The script is predictable: 'Why do things always screw up for me? Why can't these things go smoothly? Would the universe go amuck if, just once, something went according to my design? Why do events always conspire to bring me mechanical failure?' Yes, I'm angry, but what are worse are my unspoken assumptions: I should not be frustrated by things like this; events and circumstances should pan out as I intend them; when I design to do something, I should be able to accomplish it without stuff messing up. I am assuming beneath it all that I am a little (?) deity – nothing should stand in my way, glitch up my purposes; these things should not happen to **me**, and so on. Of course, it's both stupid – and yet godless, for I am assuming a deity-status that is not mine. A little touch of everyday idolatry. So if we have any penchant for clear thinking at all, we should never hesitate to confess how 'great' our guilt is. Thankfully, Yahweh is committed (cf. 'on account of your name') to pardoning such a massive mess.

Another provision consists of *assurance and friendship* (vv. 12-14). This provision is for the man who 'fears

Yahweh' (v. 12) and, in the plural, for 'those fearing him' (v. 14). When the OT text mentions 'fearing Yahweh' one often hears a follow-up like: 'Now that doesn't mean being afraid of the Lord'; then someone might add, 'It's an OT way of expressing trust in the Lord.' A nice way of emasculating the idea, as if there is a fear without fear. No, I'm not saying it's an equivalent to craven terror, but texts like Psalm 119:120, Jeremiah 5:22, and Malachi 2:5 ought to keep us from draining all the knee-knocking out of it.[4] If it connotes trust we must always remember it is a *trembling* trust.

The assurance to these Yahweh-fearers is partly – see verse 12b – much the same as in verses 8-9: clear direction. But then verse 13 adds a general assurance that this Yahweh-fearer will himself enjoy God's goodness and 'his seed' (his descendants) will enjoy life in the land. But then David adds even more in verse 14, and we need to pay special attention to this 'more'.

For one thing, believers enjoy 'the closeness of Yahweh'. The word is *sôd*. It can mean 'council', a group of persons sitting together to confer (cf. Gen. 49:6), and their being bound together in a council suggests ideas of intimacy or fellowship (cf. Ps. 55:14; Job 29:4) and a place where confidences or secrets may be shared (cf. Prov. 20:19). Hence *sôd* here speaks of 'close, intimate communion between God and his people'.[5] So much for cold, distant, detached Old Testament religion. But there is more to the

---

4   In Malachi 2:5, 'fearing' Yahweh stands in parallel with 'being shattered' (*ḥātat*) before His name.

5   Allen P. Ross, *A Commentary on the Psalms: Volume 1 (1-41)*, Kregel Exegetical Library (Grand Rapids: Kregel, 2011), 603.

'more'. Perhaps we could say that besides intimacy (v. 14a) there is also insight (v. 14b): 'his covenant he makes known to them.' The text is a bit difficult and my translation a bit awkward, but I believe it captures the thought. What does it mean to 'make known his covenant'? A believer already stands in covenant relation to Yahweh. So it seems to me that if Yahweh 'makes known' His covenant to him, it means He leads him to grasp something of the breadth and length and height and depth (cf. Eph. 3:18) of that covenant relationship – that Yahweh 'un-packs' more and more of the richness of that covenant relation. And part of that must involve seeing far more of the sheer wonder and delight of God's own nature and ways with His people. It's why the God of the Bible is not boring, for as 'the fountain of living waters' (Jer. 2:13) He is always refreshing us with striking and comfort-laden views of Himself.

An analogy may help. During the 1950s Winston Churchill was one famous fellow, and wealthy folks would vie with one another to have the Churchills come and stay with them. But that was no light undertaking. As Christopher Catherwood notes, such a visit meant over one hundred suitcases, a vast retinue of valets, bodyguards, private secretaries, research assistants, and various other members of the family.[6] In short, a Churchill epiphany may involve far more than a host may have initially imagined. In the same way (only in a positive sense) Yahweh's covenant with His people in which He promises to be God to them (Gen. 17:7) involves far more than we can imagine, and it

---

6   Christopher Catherwood, *Churchill: The Greatest Briton* (London: Sevenoaks, 2018), 146.

requires an ongoing tutorial for the living God to show us all it means for our understanding and security.

The alphabet isn't finished and so David presses on to speak of the **pressures** that he faces (vv. 15-22). First off, he speaks of what he might call 'the paradox of my situation' (vv. 15-17). On the one hand he has a firm confidence – his eyes are fixed on Yahweh, 'he [emphatic] will bring out my feet from the net' (v. 15). (Perhaps he says this because of the provisions he reviewed in vv. 8-14). But with the confidence there is desperation: 'for I am alone and afflicted' (v. 16). Here is that same mix of confidence and petition that we saw in verses 2-3. And sometimes, verse 17 may suggest, the loneliness and affliction may get worse before relief comes: 'they have enlarged the troubles of my heart.' Sometimes in the middle of that nexus of trust and trouble, the trouble will intensify and multiply. We don't like to talk this way, at least not in church, but sometimes when we trust (v. 15) and pray (v. 16) things get much worse (v. 17).

Then David speaks, in verses 18-19, of what he could call 'the complexity of my trouble'. From what follows it's clear that he is still leaning on Yahweh, for he says, 'I have taken refuge in you' (v. 20) and, 'I have waited for you' (v. 21),[7] but he's still facing a double trouble:

Look on my affliction and my trouble
– and forgive all my sins.
Look on my enemies, for they have multiplied,
    and they hate me with vicious hatred (vv. 18-19).

---

7   Note that verse 20 picks up the shame/be ashamed theme from verses 2-3.

There is a sense in which he cannot get away from his sins – his concern over them hangs over the psalm. 'Do not remember the sins of my youth' (v. 7); 'you must pardon my guilt' (v. 11); and now, 'forgive all my sins' (v. 18). Oh, it's true he has enemies and he is fully aware of their fanatical hatred (v. 19). But he is not so simple that he thinks his only trouble is on the 'outside'. He is not so naïve to fall into the 'if only' trap. 'If only Yahweh takes out my enemies....' David would agree with Charlotte Elliott's hymn: 'Fightings and fears *within*, without.' He doesn't make the mistake of forgetting the traitor within but keeps his own failure and folly in front of him as well.

And yet the pressures are not David's alone, for in verse 22 we could say he speaks of 'the need of your people': 'Redeem Israel, O God, from all his troubles.' I see no reason why this verse could not have come from David himself, though it may have come from a Psalm 'editor' when the Psalms were being compiled. Either way, there's a certain recognition involved – that what the psalm depicts of the need of the king is the same kind of need the whole covenant people have. Because the need is similar, the whole people can take an *individual* prayer and pray it as a *corporate* prayer. This partly explains why the Psalms have such a grip on God's people even in our own day – because believers intuitively sense that there is a certain *transferability* from the stuff of the psalm to the stuff of their own lives.

I remember an incident when I was a lad of six or seven. We lived in a small western Pennsylvania town, where my father was pastor of the United Presbyterian Church. Sometimes on Sunday evenings we joined together for 'union' services with other congregations in town. And on one of these nights in the Methodist church there was an informal time afterwards in which a visiting musician was leading some singing. He accompanied the singing on his accordion. (At that time, an accordion was as 'cool' as a guitar today.) He introduced a song he wanted us to sing and asked if any of us knew it. I think it was one of those 'bouncier' pieces that the Methodists seemed to prefer. So I raised my hand and told him, 'I'm a United Presbyterian, but I know it.' Well, that's it, isn't it? If it's worth singing, it doesn't need to be locked up with a bunch of Methodists. Surely a 'UP' can take it up and sing it as well. There's that 'carry over'. And the people who read and sang the psalms knew that they had this 'carry-over-ability' – that what the individual believer (or even the king) sang was likely the same sort of thing they needed to sing and to pray.

Of course, we may crave something far more orderly than a rag-tag plea about deliverance, forgiveness, and guidance with nothing but the dry bones of the Hebrew alphabet to hold the mix together. But this complexity, this messiness, is likely closer to real Christian experience than some nauseous discussion on 'four steps to the recovery of Christian equilibrium'. So let's stick with it.

Psalm 26

Of David.

(1) Set me in the clear, Yahweh,
    for **I** have walked in my whole-heartedness
    and **in Yahweh** I have trusted
    – I will never slip.

(2) Try me, Yahweh, and put me to the test,
    assess my affections and my heart.

(3) Indeed, your covenant love stands right before my eyes,
    and I have walked along in your faithfulness.

(4) I have not sat with worthless men,
    and I will not go with hypocrites.

(5) I hate the assembly of evil-doers,
    and I will not sit with the wicked.

(6) I wash my hands in innocence
    and go round your altar, Yahweh,

(7) to join in with the voice of thanksgiving
    and to tell about all your wonderful deeds.

(8) O Yahweh, I love the refuge of your house,
    even the place where your glory dwells.

(9)   Do not gather me up with sinners,
       or my life with men who shed blood,

(10) who have an evil scheme in hand
       and their right hand is full of bribes.

(11) But I, I will go on walking in my whole-heartedness
       – ransom me and show grace to me.

(12) My foot stands on level ground;
       in the assemblies I will bless Yahweh.

Living the Separated Life

2

My first overt encounter with Psalm 26 came when I was in fifth grade. Our teacher set aside a little time one day per week at the first of the day when each student was to bring a (hopefully) memorized Bible verse beginning with the letter of the alphabet chosen for that day. (Okay, so it was a public school and I'm sure that if some parents wanted their child excused from this exercise, he/she would have been. But no one got their bowels contorted over any church-and-state issues or protested, demanding equal time for the godless). On this occasion I needed a 'J' verse, and I remember my mother pointing me to Psalm 26:1, in the AV/KJV, of course:

> Judge me, O LORD; for I have walked in mine integrity: I have trusted also in the LORD; therefore I shall not slide.

While other kids may have gotten off cheap with 'Jesus wept,' I came through with Psalm 26.

Now I suppose it is fallacious to assume that a psalmist, like David, would break down his psalm like a twenty-first century interpreter. Instead, I rather imagine he is sometimes aghast at our efforts, as if to say, 'Look at what that expositor has done to my psalm!' Still, if David were speaking in the first person, I would wager that in Psalm 26 he would say, 'Now I want you to note my request (v. 1), my reasoning (vv. 2-10), and my resolve (vv. 11-12).' Let's pretend it is so.

First, then, David says, Here is **my request** (v. 1):

Set me in the clear, Yahweh,
for **I** have walked in my whole-heartedness,
and **in Yahweh** I have trusted
– I will never slip.

'Set me in the clear' – that is what David means when the older version says, 'Judge me.' It means, 'Show that I am in the right,' or 'Make clear that I am in the right with you.' He is doubtless thinking of worthless men and evildoers (cf. vv. 4-5) who accuse and denounce him. And he wants Yahweh to vindicate him before his accusers.

We'll come back to this. But we need to note that, already in verse 1, David includes a bit of rational argumentation for why Yahweh should set him in the clear. He mentions both his lifestyle ('I have walked in my whole-heartedness') and his faith ('in Yahweh [emphatic] I have trusted') in support of his petition. This may make us nervous. But we need to be clear about what David is claiming; otherwise things get confused. It's like that football game between South Carolina and West Virginia in November 1953. It was getting dark and fog was settling in on the West Virginia stadium. The South Carolina coach could not see the scoreboard clock to see how much time was left in the game. So he grabbed a student manager and said, 'Son, go find out what the time is.' The fellow ran off and returned quickly to say, 'Coach, it's twenty minutes after four.'[1] Not the time the coach had in mind.

Hence we must be clear about this 'whole-heartedness', or 'integrity' (in the ESV), or 'blameless life' (NIV), here in verse 1. I have translated *tōm* the way I have because the basic idea suggests 'to be whole, complete,' or, as we might say, 'all there.' When David claims such whole-heartedness, he is not touting some concocted perfection but an overall consistency, not a sinless record but a godly disposition. One might say he is not claiming to be without fault but without apostasy.

So David asks Yahweh to 'judge' him, to set him in the clear, to show that he stands under Yahweh's approval. Enemies or pseudo-friends may critique, berate, or condemn him, but David appeals beyond them to Yahweh for a true verdict (and probably one that would be unmistakably clear to onlookers). That is always the path of safety and especially of freedom. Paul faced a similar sort of grime at Corinth (1 Cor. 4:1-5). Some there were evaluating Paul and his ministry not in line with his proper task (vv. 1-2) but in terms of externals, his

---

1   Tom Price, *Tales from the University of South Carolina Gamecocks Locker Room* (New York: Skyhorse, 2015), 153.

lack of impressiveness and charisma, and so on (cf. 2 Cor. 10:10). But Paul puts little stock in their assessments (1 Cor. 4:3), not because he is above criticism but because he can recognize criticism leveled on fallacious grounds. Indeed, Paul says he doesn't judge himself. Neither the Corinthians' disappointment in him nor his own self-assessment matter (vv. 3-4a), for – and here Paul steps right into freedom – 'It is the Lord who judges me' (v. 4b). And Jesus' assessment will be far more accurate than men's (v. 5) and, quite likely, much kinder!

I remember as a young lad having a pair of jeans that my mother had patched up extensively. She took material from even older jeans and sewed huge patches over the knees of these jeans and another big one across the rump area. Why all the effort at repair is beyond me! But I loved wearing those jeans, because I didn't have to be careful with them. I always had a subjective feeling of abandon and freedom when wearing them. Grass stains didn't matter; sliding in dirt on the baseball field didn't matter. They gave me such a sense of freedom.

I'm convinced that's what Paul felt when he wrote, 'It is the Lord who judges me.' Some of the Lord's servants need to grasp this. No, not that we are above all criticism, but there are some of Jesus' servants who get battered with carping criticism, sometimes on primarily frivolous matters, often from Christ's professing people, and it disheartens, discourages, and distresses them no end. And there's no magic evaporation process for all that. But Paul – and implicitly, David – recognized that the assessments of mere men and even one's own evaluations don't count for much. It is the true and likely kinder judgment of the Lord that sets us free from all such rubbish.

Now we move to the bulk of the psalm and what David might call **my reasoning** (vv. 2-10), where he presses home the sincerity of his discipleship as a kind of argument for why Yahweh should 'set me in the clear'.

He begins by noting *the consistency I show* (vv. 2-3). Part of this 'consistency' sits below the visibility line – he is conscious of the sincerity of his 'affections' and 'heart'. But that is something Yahweh can test. There is this internal area, this 'deep' arena, and David claims it is anchored on Yahweh. But then there is something that *is* visible (v. 3), which gives actual evidence that the internal is in proper order:

> Your covenant love stands right before my eyes,
> and I have walked along in your faithfulness.

David seems to say that Yahweh's covenant love or grace is the vision that directs his living and that Yahweh's faithfulness has always been the arena of his experience. I agree with Alexander that *'emeth* (sometimes translated 'truth') has the sense of reliability or 'faithfulness' here (as in Pss. 30:9; 71:22; 91:4).[2] Note that he does not say, 'I have walked along in my faithfulness,' but 'in *your* faithfulness'. Is he not then speaking of all his to-date experiences of God's faithfulness to him? Is his statement not the equivalent of saying, 'I have been enjoying your faithfulness to me all along the way'? It implies that if

---

2   J. A. Alexander, *The Psalms Translated and Explained* (1864; reprint ed., Grand Rapids: Zondervan, n.d.), 114, 118.

David has remained consistent (and he is claiming that), it is because experiencing God's faithfulness has kept him so.

Then David says, But there is also *the company I shun* (vv. 4-5). He mentions worthless men (lit., 'men of emptiness'), hypocrites (lit., 'those who conceal themselves,' that is, their real thoughts), evil-doers, and the wicked. He does not 'hang out' ('sit') with them, does not bask in their camaraderie.[3] That seems to be the sense. This 'separation' can lead to a certain loneliness (cf. Jer. 15:17). There can be a certain cost to pay, as 1 Peter 4:4 suggests: they can't conceive why you don't drown yourself in the same debauchery they crave; it drives them nuts and they get so angry and vicious over it that they malign and bad-mouth you. But the fact remains that part of 'walking in whole-heartedness' (v. 1) means you 'hate the assembly of evil-doers' (v. 5a). Holiness requires hatred.

This point reminds me of an episode in the War between the States. There was a gallant Federal officer who was boldly riding his white horse in front of his men and under fire, urging his men to fight on. The Confederate general, Richard Ewell, was so impressed with this opponent's

---

3 Any assertion like this always causes someone to object, 'But Jesus associated with sinful and evil people.' One answer to that is: Jesus is Jesus and you are you. But perhaps Alexander Maclaren has a better answer: 'None comes so near to sinful man as the sinless Christ; and if He had not been ever "separate from sinners," He would never have been near enough to redeem them. We may safely imitate His free companionship, which earned Him His glorious name of their Friend, if we imitate His remoteness from their evil' (*The Psalms*, 3 vols. [reprint ed., Minneapolis: Klock & Klock, 1981], 1:254).

bravado and gallantry that he went down the Confederate lines, ordering his men not to fire on the audacious Federal officer. However, finally this brave enemy soldier had fallen. Ewell's superior, Stonewall Jackson, asked if this story (which he had heard) was true. Ewell admitted it was and commented on how magnificent the Federal's bearing had been. Jackson cut him off with a show of wrath: 'Never do such a thing again, General Ewell. This is no ordinary war. The brave Federal officers are the very kind that must be killed. Shoot the brave officers and the cowards will run away and take the men with them.'[4] Sounds brutal and is. But Jackson was trying to get Ewell's head screwed on right, as if to say: This is war; that is the enemy; your job is not to mollycoddle him but to get rid of him.

God's people need a Psalm 26 to say something similar to them. We are so smothered in our culture and in the church with sugary pronouncements about needing to 'accept' everyone that we may lose the hostility we're meant to keep! There's an expression some southerners in the US use when someone wants to get in the good graces of someone else – they speak of 'kissin' up' to them. David says he has not done that; he has not cozied up or 'kissed up' to crafty (cf. v. 4b) folks who hate God, His laws, and His people.

Next David mentions *the worship I love* (vv. 6-8). David's whole-heartedness appears not only in his separation (vv. 4-5, the 'negative' pole) but also in

---

4   Burke Davis, *They Called Him Stonewall* (New York: Fairfax, 1954), 192.

his devotion (vv. 6-8, the 'positive' pole). If he shuns fellowship with evil, he nevertheless craves the exercises of worship. In this segment he speaks of preparation (v. 6) and declaration (v. 7) and affection (v. 8). Moses and Aaron and Aaron's sons would wash hands and feet at the laver in the tabernacle before serving at the altar or tent (Exod. 40:30-32). Perhaps David is thinking of an analogous sort of preparation before he goes joyfully around Yahweh's altar (v. 6b) in celebration (cf. Ps. 43:3-4). His celebration, however, consists in grateful, verbal declaration of Yahweh's marvelous deeds (v. 7). Notice how Psalm 103 is a model of this, or Psalm 139 in a more pensive mode. The 'rehearsal' pattern in, for example, Romans 8:32-34, provides a NT sample. The praise centers on Yahweh's saving deeds, not on our feelings and experience. All of this moves him to simple exclamation: 'O Yahweh, I love the refuge of your house' (v. 8a).[5] Here in verse 8 we are moving in the orbit of other psalms that express such appetite and craving for Yahweh's house (see Pss. 42–43; 63; 84; or even, next in line, Ps. 27).

We may cynically wonder if there are still believers like this who are semi-delirious over public worship. And the answer is Yes. I've met them, and they were not engaging in self-advertising at all. For almost five years it was my privilege to preach at the Sunday evening worship services at First Presbyterian Church in Columbia, South Carolina. I recall how any number of times someone

---

5   Allen Ross strongly prefers 'refuge' in rendering $m\bar{a}\ 'ôn$ (see *A Commentary on the Psalms: Volume 1 (1-41)*, Kregel Exegetical Library [Grand Rapids: Kregel, 2011], 616).

would say something like: 'I simply *love* the Lord's Day. We get to begin the day in morning worship and then, like a proper book-end, we get to close it with evening worship.' It was something of that Psalm 26 affection for the Lord's house and what we get to do there.

And then David says he also wants Yahweh to 'set him in the clear' because of *the end I fear* (vv. 9-10):

Do not gather me up with sinners,
or my life with men who shed blood,
who have an evil scheme in hand
and their right hand is full of bribes.

You can pick up his main concern in the main verb – 'do not gather up.' He does not want to share the destiny of these murdering, scheming, bribing sinners. He is likely thinking in terms of final judgment, and he does not want to share in the divine repudiation that awaits them.

There's a contemporary attitude (I think it's even oozed into the church) that operates on a God-in-our-own-image principle and would likely pooh-pooh David's concern here. 'Well, of course, God as we conceive of Him, the merciful, soft, sentimental, mushy god we prefer, would never bring David to share such judgment.' Which would mean that David's anxiety here is just a tad ridiculous. But Jesus does not seem to agree; He seems to tell us that it's very proper to have such fears (Luke 12:4-5, RSV):

I tell you, my friends, do not fear those who kill the body, and after that have no more that they can do. But I will warn you whom to fear: fear him who, after he has killed, has power to cast into hell; yes, I tell you, fear him!

It seems to me that David's fear in verses 9-10 is very much in line with Luke 12:5. Indeed, our proper fears can be salutary.

In June of 1914 the Hapsburg Archduke Franz Ferdinand was scheduled to attend army maneuvers in the Bosnian mountains and, as a goodwill gesture to the South Slav population, he decided to pay a ceremonial visit to Sarajevo, the Bosnian capital. As another show of goodwill, he asked that 'the troops normally lining the streets for security during an Imperial visit be dispensed with.'[6] Except for a scattering of local policemen, the crowds would have fairly free access to the Archduke. That's why when the motorcade was returning from City Hall, Gavrilo Princip, a native Bosnian, was able to step forward and fire two pistol shots into the Archduke and his wife respectively. What if the Archduke had allowed some fear to hold sway and to have retained the usual tight security? He would likely have lived, and, though World War I would probably not have been cancelled, it may have been delayed.

It seems to me that David's 'fear' in verses 9-10 is a good fear, a proper fear, a faithful fear. If he is to be vindicated, he must not share in the destiny of the godless. What's wrong with making that a part of our prayers? What's wrong with a holy fear?

That then – in verses 2-10 – is what we've said David would call 'my reasoning'. His prayer is marshalling reasons for why Yahweh should 'set (him) in the clear'

---

6   Robert K. Massie, *Dreadnought* (New York: Random House, 1991), 858.

(v. 1), why Yahweh should be committed to his welfare. And, rightly understood, he is not engaging in merit-grubbing but simply arguing on the basis of the consistency of his life.

Finally, David closes the psalm by speaking of **my resolve** (vv. 11-12). What does he do now? Where, we might say, does he go from here? I want to pay special attention to verse 11a here. Note how here he comes back to the 'whole-heartedness' theme of verse 1. He vows, 'But I, I will go on walking in my whole-heartedness.' The 'I' is emphatic (I've tried to reflect that in the repetition in my translation), just as it is in verse 1. And, of course, we have the same verb, 'walk;' only in verse 1 'walk' is in a 'tense' that sums up the pattern of his life up to that time. In verse 11, the verb is in a different form, which implies what he intends to *go on doing*. I *have* walked in whole-heartedness (v. 1), and I intend to *go on* living like that (v. 11a). His petition is essentially the same (v. 11b) – that has not changed; nor has his determination to go on living in faithfulness to Yahweh.

You might have hoped for something more scintillating, well, something more climactic. But sometimes, after committing our case to God, there's no need to change how we've been living, except to go on living that way.

I know I've used it before in some book or other, but it fits again. I remember our college Dean and Greek professor telling us once in class about some Christian fellow in the early centuries A.D., who was plowing a field with his ox or whatever. Some excited, super-charged Christian brother came by, one who was apparently struck by the imminence of Jesus' second coming and asked our plowing friend what he would do if he knew that Jesus would return, say, in the next hour. The man looked down the field, pointed, and said, 'I'd finish the furrow.' Maybe you need to realize that. Amid your troubles and prayers, the Lord is not necessarily calling you to 'higher ground' or to heroic efforts; maybe He simply wants you to 'go on walking' in your whole-heartedness.

The Beauty of the Lord

Spring 1951. A young centerfielder named Willie Mays was playing baseball for the Minneapolis Millers, a minor league affiliate of the (then) New York Giants. The Millers had traveled to Sioux City, Iowa, for an exhibition game but had the day off. Willie Mays went to the movies. He liked westerns, and he liked to go by himself. He found he could relax at the movies. But on this spring day, mid-way through the movie, the lights came on and a man came onstage and announced, 'If Willie Mays is in the audience, would he please report immediately to his manager at the hotel?'[1] Why stop the movie? Why the special treatment? Because Willie Mays was a special baseball player (as future years would prove) and he was batting a prodigious .477 for Minneapolis and the bigwigs in New York felt that the major league team desperately needed him. Hence the

1   James S. Hirsch, *Willie Mays: The Life, the Legend* (New York: Scribner, 2010), 77.

special treatment: stop the movie in Sioux City to get him to New York.

Now Psalm 27:4 is like Willie Mays, only it's a text – a stellar text. Ordinarily I wouldn't 'stop the movie' to give it special attention, but I fear that if I discussed it adequately along with the whole Psalm, the exposition might become inordinately long. It's a jewel of a text in itself, and I think we'd do well to stop and ask just what David may have been thinking of, when he spoke of gazing on 'the beauty of Yahweh' in the house of Yahweh. His words are:

> One thing [emphatic] I have asked from Yahweh
> – that's what I will seek:
> that I might dwell in the house of Yahweh
> all the days of my life
> to gaze on the beauty of Yahweh
> and to seek out (things) in his temple (Ps. 27:4).

Here David states his preoccupation and passion in terms of where (in the house of Yahweh) and what (to gaze on the beauty of Yahweh). Now there's a slight problem, for the 'house of Yahweh' in David's time seemed to be a split-up affair. The bulk of the tabernacle worship center was in Gibeon, while the ark of the covenant, which David had recovered (see 2 Sam. 6), was in Jerusalem in a special tent David had pitched for it (see 2 Chron. 1:3-4; also 1 Chron. 16:37-42; 21:28-29). But when David worshiped, say at Gibeon, he would still remember the Exodus tabernacle and its furnishings; he would, we must remember, never have seen into the Most Holy Place nor would he ever have entered the Holy Place – but he would know what was there. I am supposing here that there were items in Yahweh's house which constituted Yahweh's 'beauty' for David. This procedure is obviously a bit imaginative, but it may help to give content to 'the beauty of the Lord', which otherwise must dissolve into a warm but nebulous emotional glow. So let's try to imagine how David would discover the Lord's beauty in the Lord's house. How would he see the beauty of the Lord there?

He could see Yahweh's beauty **in His condescension**. The fact that there simply *was* a tabernacle spoke volumes. It was God's tent, but His tent was always a tent among His people.

The very existence of the tabernacle should have always been suggestive to an Israelite. One can trace it all in the Book of Exodus, where it is clear that the God of 3:5 and 19:21 is also the God of 25:8 – that is, the God of the bush who will rescue His people from slavery and the God of the hill who declares to His people His Law is also the God of the tent who dwells in the midst of His people, with His tent among their tents. Indeed, the climax of the Book of Exodus is not at the sea (ch. 14) nor on the mountain (ch. 19) but in the tent (chs. 25ff.). The pinnacle of Exodus is 25:8, 'And they shall make for me a sanctuary, and I shall dwell in their midst.'

The Westminster Confession of Faith (7.1) says that we can never have any blessedness from God except 'by some voluntary condescension on God's part'. That's what one sees in the tabernacle and the Book of Exodus: the God who delivers His people and demands of His people is the God who dwells among His people. The high and holy One stoops down and, as it were, pitches His tent among their tents. That is the testimony of Exodus 25-40 – *God cannot get close enough to His people.* He must be among them.

I have always been impressed by that account of Charles XII of Sweden, when leading an expedition against the Russians at Narva. It was really too late in the year for such affairs; it was November-ish and there was rain and sleet and snow. It was all mud and muck and misery, and Charles was leading his men through it all. But when the army camped for the night in this morass, there was no royal tent where Charles and his special cronies enjoyed some degree of comfort. No, the king slept among his troops, receiving, as one account has it, 'the rain and the snow in his face.' Well, there's something beautiful about that.

That is, I should think, part of what David sees in the tabernacle. And it points on to the One who 'became flesh and pitched his tent among us' (John 1:14), the One who said, 'If anyone loves me, he will keep my word, and my Father will love him and we will come and make our home with him' (John 14:23). Yahweh, then, is the God of the flaming bush and of the smoking mountain, but He's also the God of the pitched tent – He has such an obsession to be among His people. And there's something beautiful about that.

David could also see Yahweh's beauty **in His revelation**. Even if David were worshiping at the tabernacle in Gibeon that was then minus the ark of the covenant, he would still have remembered that the ark had previously rested in the innermost section of the tabernacle, the 'most holy place'. That sacred, gold-covered, hollow, cherubim-decked box contained the two copies of Yahweh's covenant Law, the ten 'words' or commandments (Deut. 10:1-5). The ark of the covenant was a standing witness that Yahweh had *revealed His will* to His people. But that 'will' was not limited to His 'moral law'. In Exodus 25:22 Yahweh tells Moses (the 'yous' are singular, referring only to Moses), 'There [at the ark] I shall come to meet you,' and 'I shall give you all my orders for the Israelites' (NJB). So the ark was the place not only of God's holy Law but of His *ongoing direction* for His people. Israel enjoys the light of Yahweh's commanding word. But how does that show 'the beauty of the Lord'?

It's beautiful if you consider the alternative. What if you are an ancient near-eastern pagan? Well, didn't they have 'law codes'? Yes, but they required no response from the people. Their laws did not originate from a revealing god. A god may approve or oversee the laws, but the laws are those of a king, like Hammurabi, and they are not for people to live by but are the king's defense of his reign, i.e., that it was just. God's Law in Israel was public law – it was meant to be lived out in the life of the people, governing their thinking and worship and relations. In paganism there was no such direction. People did not receive guidelines for their behavior from the gods. In paganism 'something could be pleasing or displeasing to the gods, but one had no measure by which to determine what would be pleasing to deity or to which deity it might be pleasing.'[2] Which might drive a pagan worshiper nuts!

---

2   John H. Walton, *Ancient Israelite Literature in its Cultural Context* (Grand Rapids: Zondervan, 1989), 88. See also Nahum Sarna, *Exploring Exodus* (New York: Schocken, 1986), 168-78.

Check the 'Prayer to Every God' in J. B. Pritchard's *Ancient Near Eastern Texts* (3rd ed., pp. 391-92). Here's a fellow who doesn't know how he has offended some god or goddess, nor what god or goddess he has offended, nor why he's getting beaten into the ground because of what he has or has not done. That's the morass of paganism; that's what life is like when you have a god who never reveals his will or has no will to reveal. But the ark of the covenant shows how different Yahweh is – in the ark is His covenant Law and at the ark He reveals everything else Israel may need to direct their lives (Exod. 25:22).

There's kindness in clarity – even if it may be severe clarity. When Harry Truman was nominated for Vice President in 1944, Republican congresswoman Claire Booth Luce reported that Truman's wife, Bess, was on his Senate payroll; she called her 'payroll Bess'. Truman explained the work his wife did, but Luce still roasted her. After Truman became President, Claire's husband, Henry Luce, asked Truman why he never invited Mrs. Luce to any White House functions. So Truman enlightened him: 'I have been in politics for thirty-five years, and everything that could be said about a human being has been said about me. But my wife has never been in politics, and she has always conducted herself in a circumspect manner. No one has a right to make derogatory remarks about Mrs. T. Your wife has said many unkind and untrue things about her. And as long as I am in residence here, she'll never be a guest in the White House.'[3] That's pretty direct. One

---

3   Paul F. Boller, Jr., *Presidential Wives* (New York: Oxford, 1988), 324-25.

might say it's brutally clear. And yet in its own way there is a certain kindness in it: whether Mr. Luce liked it or not, there was no fuzziness; he knew where he stood; he could at least deal with it.

How much more with a God who puts His commands and His words out in the open for His people. No guessing about what pleases Him. Not that He reveals all truth, just all necessary truth. But He has put it in writing, and so we have opportunity for meditation, digestion, and appropriation (Ps. 1:2). There's something beautiful about a God who speaks.

David may also have seen Yahweh's beauty **in His sustenance**. David would not have seen into the 'holy place' of the tabernacle, but he would surely know that on the north side of that compartment sat the table where 'the bread of the Presence' was placed (see Exod. 25:23-30), where fresh loaves replaced the old weekly (cf. Lev. 24:5-9). In fact, David had had his own experience with that bread. When he was hustling to escape Saul's clutches, he had gone to Ahimelech the priest and asked for bread for himself and his men (1 Sam. 21:1-6). Ahimelech had none except the bread that was coming off the table in the holy place. A provision David surely remembered. But the bread in the holy place would also surely conjure up memories of Israel's wilderness journey and Yahweh's provision of manna for Israel 'morning by morning' during that time (Exod. 16, esp. v. 21). That table in the holy place speaks of Yahweh as the sustainer of Israel.

All this we tend to take in stride, but such was not the case in paganism. In paganism the principle was that man was to serve the gods and sustain the gods. In the

Babylonian *Enuma Elish* man is made so that he/they can relieve the lesser gods of the drudge work they have to do for the higher gods. The idea that man must tend to and sustain the gods comes out clearly in the way the images of deities were pampered and 'fed' and cared for.[4] In paganism man holds up the deities, in biblical faith God sustains His people. We meet this revolutionary idea early on, in Genesis 1:29. God told man that He had given him plants and trees, and adds, 'You shall have them for food.' So here is a God not dependent on me, a God who doesn't 'eat' or need caloric intake (Ps. 50:12-13), but rather One who 'prepares a table before me' (cf. Ps. 23:5) and therefore One who sustains me, who holds me up, who gives what I need to keep on going. There's something beautiful about getting a glimpse of the manna-giving God in the house of the Lord.

Finally, we might say David saw the beauty of the Lord **in His atonement**. The altar of sacrifice stood there in the tabernacle court. It was the first piece of furniture David or any worshiper would see on entering the court. In the burnt-offerings the priests would throw the blood against the altar (Lev. 1:5). That bronze altar in the outer court so much as announced to all comers: 'There can be no true worship apart from atonement, sacrifice, and blood.'

The good news, however, is that the altar was Yahweh's gift. The key OT text here is Leviticus 17:11: 'And I, I have given it [sacrificial blood] to you upon the altar to make atonement for your lives.' Note: 'I have given it.'

---

4   See, e.g., *ABD*, 3:377-78.

This OT sacrificial 'system' is not some way of buying off God but is a provision of His grace. And at this altar where sacrificial blood is shed one sees the beauty of the Lord, in that here I see clearly that He deals with my guilt. There is an altar of sacrifice, where blood is shed, where a life can be substituted for my life. David can surely see the beauty of the Lord because he sees an altar where guilt is paid for by the blood of a substitute. If I may mix my time-lines, is there anything more beautiful than the risen Jesus pointing you to His empty cross and quoting Leviticus 17:11 to you – 'I have given it to you ... to make atonement for your life'?

Perhaps this exposition is too imaginative. But if David's one holy passion was to dwell in the house of Yahweh to gaze on the beauty of Yahweh, I think we need to think through what kind of beauty he found there. It wasn't simply a warm, fuzzy feeling. Hence these suggestions. But we also know that the Lord's beauty overflows the bounds of the 'sanctuary', and it's important that we have eyes to see it. I still find moving that anecdote Iain Murray tells of a mid-nineteenth century John Murray in Scotland. A fellow clansman visited him one day and was asked to stay for the family's mid-day meal of potatoes and salt. The guest expressed his sympathy with Mr. Murray – he was not criticizing – when he noted that 'the potatoes are so poor'. Yet Mr. Murray replied, 'There is not one of them on which I do not see the beauty of the Blood.'[5] So much depends on what you are able to see, and John Murray

---

5   Iain H. Murray, 'Life of John Murray,' in *Collected Writings of John Murray: Volume 3* (Edinburgh: Banner of Truth, 1982), 10n.

saw his scant repast as part of the bounty purchased by his Savior. Perhaps even in the poor fare of a mid-day meal we can also see the beauty of the Lord.

Psalm 27

Of David.

(1) Yahweh (is) my light and my salvation
    – whom should I fear?
  Yahweh (is) the stronghold of my life
    – whom should I dread?

(2) When evildoers came near to (attack) me,
    to eat up my flesh,
  my adversaries and my enemies,
  they were the ones who stumbled and fell.

(3) Should an army camp against me
    my heart will not fear;
  should war rise up against me
    – in this situation I will go on trusting.

(4) **One thing** I have asked from Yahweh
    – that's what I will seek:
  that I might dwell in the house of Yahweh
    all the days of my life
  to gaze on the beauty of Yahweh
    and to seek out (things) in his temple;

(5) for he will hide me in his lair
    in the day of trouble;
  he will conceal me in the cover of his tent;
  he will lift me up high on a rock.

(6) And now my head will be high above my enemies
        all around me,
    and I will sacrifice in his tent sacrifices
        with joyful shouts;
    I will sing, yes, I will make music to Yahweh.

(7) Hear, Yahweh! I cry out loud;
    and show grace to me and answer me.

(8) To you my heart has said –
        'Seek [plural] my face!' –
    'Your face, Yahweh, I will seek.'

(9) Don't cover up your face from me;
    don't turn away your servant in anger;
    you have been my help!
    Don't leave me and don't forsake me,
        O God of my salvation.

(10) For my father and my mother have forsaken me,
    but **Yahweh** will gather me in.

(11) Teach me your way, Yahweh,
    and lead me on a level path
        because of those lurking for me.

(12) Don't give me over into the desire of my adversaries,
    for false witnesses have risen up against me
    – violent ones too!

(13) I have believed I will see the goodness of Yahweh
        in the land of the living.

(14) Wait for Yahweh!
    Be strong and let your heart be bold!
    Yes, wait for Yahweh!

Paradoxical Psalm

I am looking at a copy of a lad's school report from 1881. One comment is: 'Conduct has been exceedingly bad. He is not to be trusted to do any one thing.' It notes that he has been late twenty times, with the addition: 'Very disgraceful.' Near the bottom of the page I read of his 'general conduct': 'Very bad – is a constant trouble to everybody and is always in some scrape or other. He cannot be trusted to behave himself anywhere.' That lad was later voted 'the greatest Briton of all time' in an extensive poll taken many years after his death, involving voters not even alive during his lifetime.[1] You can guess – Winston Churchill. How could such a scurvy urchin also come to carry off such laurels? Well, it's a bit of a paradox. Like Psalm 27. Some critics think it must have been

---

1   Christopher Catherwood, *Churchill: The Greatest Briton* (London: Sevenoaks, 2018), 5, 15.

two psalms since the first part radiates such marvelous assurance (vv. 1-6) but the second (vv. 7-12) such urgent need. How can these both be part of a single psalm? For now, let's assume we've got a paradox and come back to this question later.

The general division of the psalm is clear: verses 1-6 go together and speak of Yahweh in the third person ('he,' etc.), while verses 7-12 are in second person address-mode ('you,' etc.) except for verse 10b.[2] Then verses 13-14 form the final note or exhortation of the psalm.

I will put the main heads in the first person as if David himself were stating them, and so in verses 1-6 he would speak of **the assurance I enjoy**. The whole tone is positive and confident.

In verses 1-3 he indicates how assurance begins. It actually begins with who Yahweh is. If He is 'light' and 'salvation' and 'stronghold', then indeed what is there to fear or dread? But such confidence is not merely a 'credal' matter, for Yahweh has shown Himself as salvation and stronghold in actual experience (v. 2):

> When evildoers came near to (attack) me,
> > to eat up my flesh,
> > my adversaries and my enemies,
> **they** were the ones who stumbled and fell.

The last two verbs should be translated as English past tenses (as NASB, NKJV), not as futures (as NIV, NRSV). He is remembering past occasions when salivating enemies

---

2   Cf. P. C. Craigie, *Psalms 1-50, Word Biblical Commentary* (Waco: Word Books, 1983), 230.

were frustrated and crushed. And such deliverances then give him a confident outlook in case any further assaults should come his way (v. 3). The root of his assurance then has come from Yahweh's being what He actually is (v. 1) and showing that character in bringing about the demise of enemies who've tried to eliminate him (v. 2).

Then we meet verse 4, which doesn't seem to have any explicit connection with verses 1-3. Here he speaks of his consuming desire:

> ... that I might dwell in the house of Yahweh
>> all the days of my life
> to gaze on the beauty of Yahweh
>> and to seek out (things) in his temple.[3]

I have already dealt with this verse in the previous chapter, where I tried to give concrete content to the 'beauty of Yahweh' that David must have seen and considered in the tabernacle worship. Clearly he has this insatiable desire for being in Yahweh's house and Yahweh's presence, an ongoing longing for communion with Yahweh. But what possible connection does or can this have with his assurance? It is not immediately clear.

It can be difficult to see connections. Once in 1864 the Confederate general, Jubal Early, was leading his troops into Maryland, intent on attacking the Federal capital, Washington. There was a fairly obscure major general named Lew Wallace (later to write *Ben Hur*), who had a

---

3   In the last line of verse 4 I am following Alec Motyer's preference of searching out solutions to life's perplexities in Yahweh's house (cf. Ps. 73:16-17); cf. his *Psalms by the Day* (Ross-shire: Christian Focus, 2016), 69.

ragtag bunch of troops who had only signed up for one hundred days of duty. They had not seen much combat, and Early's troops all but blew them away at Frederick, Maryland. Wallace received some reinforcements and at Monocacy Junction he dug in. His defensive line was stretched thin; he had only 6,000 troops to face Early's 14,000. The battle was ferocious, went on all day, with lots of hand-to-hand combat, with the Federals taking 1,900 casualties and deaths. A clear and decisive defeat. So what does that have to do with anything? Well, in his later *Memoirs*, General Grant indicated that 'by the defeat of the troops under him', General Wallace had made a larger contribution than others do by victories, for holding off the Confederates for that bloody day meant that General Early arrived a day late at Washington, because by that time troops Grant had sent as reinforcements had arrived and Early realized he had to return to Virginia.[4] It was a defeat that saved a city, though that may not have been obvious at the time.

I think verse 4 is a bit like that – one may wonder what it has to do with assurance. But the answer seems to be that his time in Yahweh's house and in Yahweh's presence actually *intensifies* his assurance, as verse 5 seems to indicate:

> [F]or he will hide me in his lair
> > in the day of trouble;
> he will conceal me in the cover of his tent;
> he will lift me up high on a rock.

---

4   Seymour Morris, Jr., *American History Revised* (New York: Broadway Books, 2010), 14-15.

The convictions of verse 5 are the fruit of his communion in verse 4. Time spent in Yahweh's presence, 'gazing on his beauty,' contemplating all that He is to His servants (see previous chapter) has a way of reinforcing assurance, of making us ever more confident that we are safe in His hands (so v. 5). Assurance intensifies in personal communion and worship.

Think also of the graphic images of verse 5. In 5a I have followed the marginal reading in the traditional Hebrew text, reading $s\bar{o}k$, used of a lion's lair (Ps. 10:9; Jer. 25:38). You may prefer the more colorless 'shelter', but 'lair' is, I think, more consoling! Thinking of Yahweh in the imagery of a lion and His servant being hidden away in His lair, well, think how safe he is! Who is going to mess with a lion? But Yahweh is also the host, responsible for the safety and protection of all His guests, and who will therefore keep them secure 'in the cover of his tent' (v. 5b). Not only that, but Yahweh will place His servant up high on a rock, far out of the reach of those wanting to besiege him (v. 5c). The lair-tent-rock images are meant to pile up on the reader to picture complete and total safety. Which is why verse 6 shows us what assurance anticipates, the joyful, glad thanksgiving for enjoying Yahweh's keeping power.

Perhaps the major 'take-away' from David's assurance section is that time spent in the house of Yahweh and in the presence of Yahweh is never wasted – it only tends to impress us more with His preserving and defending work. The Lord of the sanctuary (v. 4) is also the God of the battlefield (vv. 5-6a) and has a way of showing up there. However, we may begin to wonder how solid all this is, for David goes right on to tell us of **the trouble I face** (vv. 7-12).

We seem to breathe different air in verses 7-12. The calm assurance of verses 1-6 gives way to an urgent plea for help and deliverance. I think that with verses 7-12 it will be more helpful to highlight some of the matters David mentions and prays about here before going on to consider the quandary of having verses 7-12 sit right alongside of verses 1-6.

Hence we can note *the obedience he practices* (vv. 8-9a). Verse 8 is perplexing:

> To you my heart has said –
>   'Seek [plural] my face' –
> 'Your face, Yahweh, I will seek.'

Obviously rough. But I assume the first and third lines go together: what David's heart has said is in the third line. The second line I take as David quoting a word of Yahweh – without introduction! The verb in the second line is plural, a word given to God's people. So I assume that David abruptly and somewhat parenthetically quotes Yahweh's command – and then in line three indicates that that is exactly what he is doing, and then goes on to plead, 'Don't cover up your face from me; don't turn your servant away in anger' (v. 9a). All this tells us that this cry in trouble is not some bit of foxhole religion. No, God has commanded him (and others) to seek Him, and David is simply being faithfully obedient to Yahweh's command and invitation.

He goes on to allude to *the assurance he possesses* (vv. 9b-10). Even in his bleak situation David has some shafts of light. One we could say is retrospective: 'you have been my help' (v. 9b). He has not fallen into this latest trouble without a history. He has had Yahweh's help in previous distresses and that gives a gleam of hope for the present one. The other assurance is prospective. He pleads not to be abandoned or forsaken and notes that his father and mother have forsaken him (v. 10a). How they had 'forsaken' him we don't know for sure. Is this a round-about way of referring to their deaths?[5] Yet in face of this 'forsakenness,' he avers that 'Yahweh [emphatic] will gather me in' (v. 10b). This sort of subtle assurance is typical of Yahweh – He has a knack of inserting little gleams of hope into our desperation.

And David also prays for *the direction he needs* (vv. 11-12). He asks Yahweh to teach him His 'way' and to lead him 'on a level path because of those lurking for me'. This 'way' is not the way of duty but of providence.[6] That is, David is not asking after any commandments he is supposed to keep but wants to know the way Yahweh intends him to take in order to come out of this trouble. He wants Yahweh to show him the pathway through the difficulties and threats he is facing. It's a sort of James 1:5 situation: you are facing diverse trials (James 1:2-4), so you come to God to ask wisdom (1:5) in order to get through them. And get through he must, for he faces the scrutiny ('those

5   Cf. Allen P. Ross, *A Commentary on the Psalms: Volume 1 (1-41)*, Kregel Exegetical Library (Grand Rapids: Kregel, 2011), 632.

6   J. A. Alexander, *The Psalms Translated and Explained* (1864; reprint ed., Grand Rapids: Zondervan, n.d.), 122.

lurking for me,' v. 11b), lying ('false witnesses,' v. 12b), and violence (v. 12c) of those eager to bring him down.

Now let's come back to the major 'problem' of verses 7-12: here David's plea in trouble seems so incompatible with his calm assurance in verses 1-6. So what are we to make of this? Some critics have thought that the two sections are so different in tone and outlook that they must've been two separate psalms by two different writers, two pieces that somehow got cobbled together at a later time.[7] Of course that won't wash. To re-cast Alexander Maclaren's argument, what later editor would dream of slapping two such different pieces together? They must have stood as parts of one psalm from the first.[8]

And why not? Is this not part of the appeal of Psalm 27? That here is a psalm that recognizes the yo-yo pattern of believing experience? Don't multitudes of the Lord's saints know what it is to move all too quickly from faith (vv. 1-6) to fear (vv. 7-12), from trust to trouble, from resting in Yahweh to pleading for rescue? Oh, it's still a matter of faith, but the abiding faith of verses 1-6 has given way to the agitated faith of verses 7-12. But doesn't it help you when you run on to a text that makes you say, 'Yes, that's the way things are! Living for Christ sometimes goes exactly like that!' And a few dense biblical critics try

---

7   Cf. A. Weiser, *The Psalms, Old Testament Library* (Philadelphia: Westminster, 1962), 245-46, 251; A. A. Anderson, *The Book of Psalms,* New Century Bible, 2 vols. (Grand Rapids: Eerdmans, 1972), 1:219.

8   Alexander Maclaren, *The Psalms*, 3 vols. (reprint ed., Minneapolis: Klock & Klock, 1981), 1:259-60.

to tell us these can't go together! Rather, this complexity of the psalm reflects the way real things are.

This matter reminds me of an historical anomaly mentioned in one of Andrew Ferguson's books. In 1864 Abraham Lincoln gave his handwritten draft of the Emancipation Proclamation to the Chicago Historical Society. The society's directors felt so honored by this that in 1868 they built a splendid, state-of-the-art repository for it on Chicago's north side, and declared this abode to be invulnerable to any disaster by man or God (the Titanic, anyone?). They dubbed it 'the perfect fireproof structure'. It burned to ashes three years later and the hand draft of the 'Proclamation' with it.[9] Completely fireproof and it burned up. It's a paradox and hard to put together.

And that's often the nature of believing experience: there is this and yet that. There's enjoying the beauty of the Lord and then there's facing an unnerving emergency. The calm of faith can become the crisis of faith. And they often occur in that sequence. How it should help the saints of God to lay hold of a text like Psalm 27, that says, 'Yes, it can be like that.' The trauma of verses 7-12 doesn't falsify the faith of verses 1-6 but deepens it.

Finally, David speaks of **the stance I take** (vv. 13-14). Verse 13 seems to be a word of testimony, while verse 14 a word of advice.[10] In verse 13 he says, 'Here's where I have

---

9   Andrew Ferguson, *Land of Lincoln* (New York: Atlantic Monthly, 2007), 79-80.

10 I am aware that some hold that verse 14 is an oracle of exhortation or salvation uttered by a priest at the sanctuary. All well and good; but we can't know that. I think it's simpler to

come to stand,' while in verse 14 he says, 'Here's where you should stand.'

The first part of verse 13 is difficult and the text a bit uncertain. It can be translated as an 'unless'-clause that is unfinished: 'Unless I believed I would see the goodness of Yahweh ...' – with the expectation that the reader would supply the unstated thought. That's the way NKJV takes it, supplying the 'missing' idea: 'I would have lost heart, unless I had believed that I would see,' etc. But the opening particle in the Hebrew could be an adverb of affirmation, in which case we could translate, 'I indeed believed that I would see the goodness of Yahweh....'[11] Either way, he stands here, even after the crud of verses 7-12, believing he will see 'the goodness of Yahweh in the land of the living'. He expects Yahweh's deliverance and help to come at some point on the calendar of this life. And he wants you to be expectant as well in what you are facing: 'Wait for Yahweh!' (v. 14). His help may yet be down the timeline; the present circumstances may be murky and messy; but there is such a thing as the goodness of Yahweh. Indeed David himself seems to say, 'I can rest here; I don't have to have all the loose ends tied up right now.' It's the stance he takes.

---

take it as the psalmist's counsel to other Israelite believers who may find themselves in his sandals.

11   See *DCH*, 4:530, and K-B, 2:524.

Psalm 28

Of David.

(1) To you, Yahweh, I am calling out;
my Rock, don't be deaf to me;
lest, if you are silent to me,
I shall be like those going down to the pit.

(2) Hear the voice of my pleas for grace,
when I cry out to you,
when I lift up my hands toward your inner sanctuary.

(3) Don't drag me off with wicked men
and with evildoers,
ones who speak peace with their neighbors
but with disaster in their heart.

(4) Give to them in line with their work
and in line with the evil of their deeds;
in line with the work of their hands give to them;
pay them back what they have dished out.

(5) For they will never discern the deeds of Yahweh,
nor the work of his hands;
he will throw them down and not build them up.

(6) Blessed be Yahweh!
For he has heard the voice of my pleas for grace.

(7)   Yahweh, my strength and my shield;
      in him my heart has trusted
            and I have been helped.
      So my heart is ecstatic
            and I will praise him with my song.

(8)   Yahweh, the strength of his people
      – and he is a stronghold of salvation
            for his anointed one.

(9)   Save your people
      and bless your possession,
      and be their shepherd
      and carry them forever.

Royal Prayer

5

I see no reason to doubt the superscription of this psalm, that it stems from David, and I assume then that when he refers to Yahweh's 'anointed one' in verse 8, he is referring to himself as the anointed covenant king. Hence it is a royal prayer. And he is praying in the midst of some emergency (vv. 1-5) which he always seemed to be facing. Some earlier expositors have thought that the psalm (along with 26 and 27) has its historical setting in Absalom's rebellion (2 Sam. 15-18). But I doubt we can be sure of that. After Absalom's rebellion had been crushed, Joab had read David the riot act for his excessive grief over Absalom's death – so much so that he failed to commend and show gratitude to his troops for their victory and protection (2 Sam. 19). Joab threatened that the troops would desert David if he didn't stop his whimpering over Absalom, which, he said, 'will be worse for you than all the disaster which has come upon you from your youth until now' (2 Sam. 19:7). I know we have to filter what we hear from Joab; he usually has his own agenda; Joab is always looking out for Joab. But there is no reason to suspect that statement. What a description: 'all the disaster that has come upon you from your youth until now.' Almost as if David's existence had been little more than a barrage of unmitigated trouble. So, when we hear him pray in Psalm 28, who knows what particular trouble he may have been in? Could have been any of his 'disasters'.

We will trace David's concerns through the psalm, and, first, we note **the silence he dreads** in verses 1-2:

> ... don't be deaf to me;
> lest, if you are silent to me,
> I shall be like those going down to the pit.
> Hear the voice of my pleas for grace....

Here is prayer that names its fears. His chief fear is that Yahweh will be 'deaf' or 'silent' — unresponsive. If Yahweh doesn't 'hear,' what then? That brings on another fear: 'I shall be like those going down to the pit.' The 'pit' (*bôr*) is sometimes synonymous with Sheol (the realm of the dead) and with death (cf. Ps. 30:3; Isa. 38:18). But there may be something more sinister here. Allen Ross is likely on target:

> Those going down to the pit are not just dying, but dying without hope. In this simile David is comparing himself to the ungodly: if his prayer goes unanswered, he will not

appear to be different. He will die as they die, without any reprieve from the LORD.[1]

And yet even as he declares these fears his prayer packs gleams of encouragement. For one thing, he calls Yahweh 'my Rock' (cf. Deut. 32:4, 15, 18, 30, 31; Ps. 95:1) with its overtones of security and stability. And perhaps more. Motyer points to Exodus 17:1-7, where the rock Moses struck became the source of life-giving water.[2] Yahweh himself was closely associated with that stricken rock (Exod. 17:6). So 'rock' may not only convey security and stability but Yahweh's sustenance and sufficiency as well.

Then there's another slice of encouragement when David speaks of lifting up his hands 'toward your inner sanctuary' (v. 2c). The inner sanctuary was the 'most holy place' of the tabernacle where the ark of the covenant sat.[3] Only the high priest went into that innermost compartment and only once a year, on the Day of Atonement (see Lev. 16). David never went in there. And yet he assumes that his prayers do! When he lifts up his hands toward Yahweh's inner sanctuary, isn't he assuming that is the case? David can never bodily enter into that

---

1   Allen P. Ross, *A Commentary on the Psalms: Volume 1 (1-41)*, Kregel Exegetical Library (Grand Rapids, Kregel, 2011), 642.

2   Alec Motyer, *Psalms by the Day* (Ross-shire: Christian Focus, 2016), 70, n22.

3   See our preceding exposition of Psalm 27:4. During part of David's reign the tabernacle was 'split up', the majority of it being in Gibeon while the ark of the covenant was in Jerusalem. But this cultic fact of life doesn't really affect our inference from verse 2 here.

sacred space, but his prayers can and do. Hence, a sliver of hope.

But let's come back to his primary fear: what if Yahweh is 'silent' or 'deaf' to his cries? What if He shouldn't 'hear'? What can be more basic or fundamental than that? Here we are at the basement floor of prayer. If Yahweh doesn't hear, it's all over. Everything depends on this. That's why we should never mumble through such parts of the Psalms. Take a look at Psalms 5:1-2; 22:1-2; 55:1-2; 61:1-2a; 83:1; and 102:1-2. These are pleas to be *heard*. And I think, if we're fairly familiar with the Psalms, that we become mentally inoculated against these opening salvos. We tend to think they are just conventional verbiage, sort of required openings before we get to the 'real stuff.' But these cries are no formality. If Yahweh doesn't hear, there is no hope.

While we were living in West Columbia, South Carolina, there was a 'Waffle House' restaurant about a mile from our home. We were surprised one December day to read about the place in the local newspaper. Seems a local man couldn't sleep and so walked to the 24-hour eatery a block from his house. Alex Bowen waited at the cash register for ten minutes for someone to take his order. No one came. He looked outside for employees but didn't find anyone. Whatever staff were supposed to be there were asleep – somewhere. Mr. Bowen decided to use the hot grill and make himself a Texas bacon cheesesteak melt. He even cleaned up after he was done. And, later in the day after conscience worked, he came back and paid for his sandwich. But there was something terribly wrong with that – a 24-hour restaurant and no one was 'there'.

So with David's prayer – if Yahweh is not there, if He is 'silent', then his prayer is the way to Nowheresville. That's why one imagines he is half-ecstatic when he calls God, in the old Authorized Version, 'O thou who hearest prayer' (Ps. 65:2). That is the main matter.

Secondly, David speaks of **the justice he craves** (vv. 3-5). Here we meet the petition proper, especially in verse 4. But first we meet the problem of the wicked (v. 3). There *are* wicked people, evildoers. Nor should we think these 'wicked' come from pagan nations; more likely, David is here thinking of folks within Israel who hate and oppose his reign as covenant king. There are two difficulties with them. They are *devious*: they 'speak peace with their neighbors but with disaster in their heart' (v. 3b). They make a good show of cozying up to the Lord's servants while in actual fact they are plotting their overthrow. They are masterful hypocrites. But then they are *dense* as well: 'they will never discern the deeds of Yahweh, nor the work of his hands' (v. 5a). Though they may know the facts of Yahweh's creating, providing, rescuing work, it doesn't 'get through' to them. They are so 'thick' that they do not acknowledge Yahweh's works or praise Him for them. They are another dismal re-run of Romans 1:21a.

So what does David do? He prays against them. Verse 4 is the primary petition:

> Give to them in line with their work
>> and in line with the evil of their deeds;
> in line with the work of their hands give to them;
> pay them back what they have dished out.

David asks for God's retribution on them. With his three-fold 'in line with' he pleads that Yahweh will pay them back in equitable proportion. This may seem too brutal to some of us in the West, who exist in a soft-headed, emotion-dripping, feeling-soaked culture. But a moment's thought tells us that David is doing nothing more than Paul would later require in Romans 12:19: Don't take vengeance yourselves; commit vengeance to God. How do you do that? You *pray* that God will take vengeance on them. Like eating your oatmeal, it's the right thing to do. That's what David is doing here – committing vengeance to God by praying that God will take them out.[4]

In late August 1944 about 2,000 American troops stationed in England were participating in a memorial service for the men killed in Normandy. A chaplain and a general spoke, but what impressed the troops far more was a regimental prayer written by Lieutenant James Morton, which began: 'Almighty God, we kneel to thee and ask to be the instrument of thy fury in smiting the evil forces that have visited death, misery, and debasement on

---

4   Sometimes one reads an expositor or commentator who says that a prayer like verse 4 is out of line with the spirit of the gospel (whatever that is) and the NT. Which is poppycock. Not only does the prayer line up with Romans 12 but with NT instances of prayers for justice (Rev. 6:9-10) or over justice (Rev. 19:1-2). With this, however, Jesus' disciples hold to Luke 6:27-28 as well – to love enemies, do good to those who hate them, and pray for those who abuse them. Is it too big a stretch to believe we are called to pray for our enemies, that God would bring them to repentance, and yet against the enemies of God's people, that God would bring them to justice? Can't we handle a bit of a paradox?

the people of the earth.'[5] It was a prayer that pleaded for justice against evil (as perceived by Americans in WW2). There's a certain rigor in such prayers, and Christians might learn from them. Sometimes believers must pray prayers that have hair on their chests.

I think Psalm 28 is instructive for Christian believers. Sometimes, depending on our circumstances, we may think 'there is nothing we can do' about the ravages of evil and wicked men. But Psalm 28 says we can do something. We can pray. We can pray against them. We can pray God will punish them. We can pray that God will take them out.

Now the tone of the psalm changes and David tells of **the praise he offers** (vv. 6-8). Yahweh has answered his prayer and so praise is in order. There is such an *exuberance* about it: 'Blessed be Yahweh!,' he exclaims (v. 6a). Then he goes on to recount how he trusted in Yahweh and has received help so that his heart is 'ecstatic' (v. 7). His praise is full of delight and given with gusto. On one occasion Franz Joseph Haydn had to apologize to Empress Marie Therese. He was setting to music the words from the Mass: 'Lamb of God, who takes away the sins of the world.' While doing this he was seized, he said, with an 'uncontrollable gladness'. Hence his apology to the empress – the certainty of God's grace had made him so happy he wrote a joyful melody for the apparently somber

---

5   See Stephen E. Ambrose, *Band of Brothers* (New York: Touchstone, 2001), 118.

words.[6] If you read verses 6-7 properly you see that David too was seized with an 'uncontrollable gladness'.

But there's more. There's such an *assurance* in this praise (v. 8). As he pours out his praise, he confesses truth about Yahweh and that truth reinforces his assurance:

> Yahweh, the strength of his people
> – and he is a stronghold of salvation
>   for his anointed one.[7]

So praise sustains confidence. It is a double confidence – Yahweh is both 'the strength of his people' and 'a stronghold of salvation for his anointed one'. The 'anointed one' is the reigning king, which, if we credit the superscription, is in this case David. There's likely a causal relation between these two matters. It would probably be right to say that Yahweh is the strength of His people *because* He is a saving stronghold for their king. As goes the king so go the people. If the king is victorious, the people are secure. With a little thought a Christian can grab hold of this. If his/her King has died, risen, sits at the right hand of God, and intercedes (Rom. 8:34), who possibly can condemn? As king, so people. In any case, here clearly what the king declares in praise willy-nilly provides additional assurance for God's people.

---

6   Patrick Kavanaugh, *The Spiritual Lives of the Great Composers* (Nashville: Sparrow, 1992), 22.

7   There's a debate about the text of verse 8a. One reading is 'to them', while another is 'to/of his people'. Since the 'them' seems to refer to God's people anyway there is no difference in meaning.

Yet there is simply such a *propriety* about this praise: 'Blessed be Yahweh! *For* he has heard the voice of my pleas for grace' (v. 6). He had asked Yahweh to hear these 'pleas for grace' in verse 2. He has done so, and for that reason praise is due. Yahweh's answer places a claim on me, and there is something desperately wrong if it doesn't elicit praise.

I ran into an odd episode during the 'Revolutionary' War in my country. One night in August 1780 Francis Marion, the 'Swamp Fox', received word that the British were holding 150 Continental soldiers captive at a plantation six miles north of his camp. The British intended to march these captives down to the South Carolina coast and incarcerate them on British prison ships there. Marion and his seventy men rode all night and attacked just before daybreak. The surprise attack was over in minutes and Marion recovered all 150 prisoners. So they gladly joined Marion's ranks? Wrong. Almost all of them decided they had had enough of fighting. They had been through a harsh winter in New Jersey and found the humid south unbearable. They had not long before been decisively whipped by the British at Camden (even their commanding general, Horatio Gates, had run away from that battlefield, rightly puncturing his bloated reputation). They saw no point in carrying on the war. So over half of them went on down to the coast and to the mercies of British prison ships; the rest pretended they were going back to their unit in North Carolina but, in fact, most deserted. And three of them stayed on to fight with

Marion.[8] It doesn't matter if you yourself are American or British (or something else) – there's something wrong with that. Rescued, delivered, set free, and they were nothing but a bunch of ingrates. Once more, Isaac Watts' lyrics should stop us in our tracks:

> O bless the Lord, my soul,
> nor let his mercies lie
> forgotten in unthankfulness,
> and without praises die.[9]

Finally, David concludes by speaking of **the people he remembers** (v. 9). He appends a prayer for Israel here at the end of the psalm:

> Save your people
> and bless your possession,
> and be their shepherd
> and carry them forever.

This is obviously a prayer for ongoing need. It was one thing for their king to be delivered and for Yahweh to show, once more, that He is 'the strength of his people' (v. 8). But Israel will face more troubles and will have more need of Yahweh's sufficiency. And what more welcome image than Yahweh as 'shepherd' who 'carries' His people? He is not some burden we have to support and carry, like pagans who toted around the images of their gods, but He is the Exodus God who always carries

---

8   John Oller, *The Swamp Fox* (Boston: Da Capo, 2016), 55-56.

9   From 'O Bless the Lord, My Soul.' See *Trinity Hymnal* (1990), No. 78.

His people (see Deut. 1:31; Isa. 46:1-4; 63:9). And how, sometimes, they need to be *carried,* for they can scarcely stand by themselves. So when serving in a congregation I often liked to take part of verse 8 and combine it with the last of verse 9 for a benediction:

> Now Yahweh, who is the strength of his people,
> be your shepherd
> and carry you – forever.

And why so? Oh, because as you look out on a congregation you see folks as needy as David's Israel. There's the couple whose adult son has recently committed suicide. There's the four or five people who suffer almost unrelenting physical pain. There's the widow who's left alone after fifty-plus years of close and cordial marriage. There are the parents who are still praying for a son who, though cordial, has been stiff-arming the gospel for years. As so often, it seems that God's Israel is barely hanging on, and they need to hear their Shepherd tell them again, 'I have made – and I will carry' (Isa. 46:4).

There's something more we should observe about this prayer: it has what we might call a prophetic spin. As David the covenant king here prays for Israel, does it not point us to the final Davidic king, Jesus, who always intercedes for His people? One thinks of Jesus' prayer for His disciples: 'Holy Father, keep them in your name, which you have given me ... keep them from the evil one' (John 17:11, 15). So the people of God still have a King who prays for them. How then can we fail to make it?

Psalm 29

A Psalm of David

(1) Give to Yahweh, O sons of God,
    give to Yahweh, glory and strength.

(2) Give to Yahweh the glory his name deserves,
    give homage to Yahweh in the splendor of (his) holiness.

(3) Yahweh's voice over the waters!
    The God of glory thunders;
    Yahweh over many waters!

(4) Yahweh's voice in power!
    Yahweh's voice in majesty!

(5) Yahweh's voice breaks cedars;
    yes, Yahweh has shattered the cedars of Lebanon.

(6) And he has made them skip around like a calf,
    Lebanon and Sirion like the young of a wild ox.

(7) Yahweh's voice is hewing up flames of fire!

(8) Yahweh's voice makes the wilderness writhe,
    Yahweh makes the wilderness of Kadesh writhe!

(9)   Yahweh's voice makes deer go into birth pangs,
      and he stripped the forests bare
      – and all in his temple say, 'Glory!'

(10) **Yahweh** sat (enthroned) at the flood,
      and Yahweh has seated (himself) as king forever.

(11) **Yahweh** will give strength to his people;
      Yahweh will bless his people with peace.

God of the Storm

6

Some friends were on holiday in Scotland. They were rummaging in second-hand bookshops and brought me back a copy of *The Covenanters in Moray and Ross* by the Rev. M. MacDonald. In that volume MacDonald passes on the story of how that scoundrel Charles II arrived in Scotland in 1650. The ship that came to the mouth of the Spey had to drop anchor away out, and a boat was used to carry passengers to shore. But there was no pier and the transfer boat could not get near enough to allow the king to disembark dry-shod. What to do? Thomas Milne, the short but robust ferryman that day, offered his back to his Majesty and told him to 'loup on'. And so the king was lugged, Milne-like, to terra firma. I would guess Charles was hoping for something with more flourish for the royal advent than a piggy-back ride to shore. Doubtless disappointing.

That is likely the way many look upon Psalm 29. Not what we were hoping for; truth be told, a bit disappointing. And why so? Oh, maybe we were hoping for more of a pain-reliever, or reading of some distressing experience of the psalmist that we could enter into. But here in Psalm 29 there seems nothing but God – and God wreaking havoc and scaring His world to death. The psalm is not about us but God – and that, sadly, tends to cool our interest. It's something like being a king and yet riding Thomas Milne to shore.

Yet Yahweh does, we might say, insist on imposing Himself on us in Psalm 29. There are eighteen uses of 'Yahweh' in these eleven verses. 'Yahweh's voice' occurs seven times. The psalm moves from the worship of Yahweh (vv. 1-2) to the revelation of Yahweh (vv. 3-9) and ends with the people of Yahweh (vv. 10-11). Or we might say it goes from exhortation to revelation and on to consolation.

We could summarize verses 1-2 as **giving orders for Yahweh's worship in heaven**. Notice several matters in the text. David calls the 'sons of God' to worship (v. 1). The phrase refers to angels or heavenly beings. The very same Hebrew phrase occurs in Psalm 89:6, of heavenly beings who can in no way compare to Yahweh. In the adjacent verses these 'sons of God' or 'heavenly beings' (ESV) form the 'assembly of the holy ones' or the 'council of the holy ones' – those who, as it were, are surrounding God's throne (Ps. 89:5, 7). Here in Psalm 29 these 'sons of God' are told in a three-fold ascending crescendo to 'Give to Yahweh!' They are to give to Him 'glory and strength' and 'the glory his name deserves'. What does that mean? It does not mean, obviously, that they can add anything to

Yahweh's majesty. It means at least to declare that glory and strength are Yahweh's and to acknowledge that they rightly belong to Him. Kidner observes that to 'give' glory and strength 'enlists the mind' (focus on the content of worship) while 'give homage' (or, 'bow down') 'enlists the will' (the matter of submission).[1] Which indicates that worship should be both thoughtful and submissive.

But now a realization should come creeping over us: if we are ordering angels to worship Yahweh with gusto, then we are not the only worshipers. This is the testimony of Psalm 103:20-21 as well:

Bless Yahweh, (you) his angels,
(you) mighty ones who do his word....
Bless Yahweh, all his hosts,
his servants who do his will.

David is speaking to the angels and celestial beings, calling them to 'bless Yahweh,' which he himself is ready to do: 'Bless Yahweh, O my soul' (v. 22). When we order angels to worship God, we can be pretty sure, I think, that they will do it.

Talking to angels may not appeal to you, but there are some of us who do so regularly. Some of us sing the 'Doxology' nearly every week in public worship. It begins:

Praise God from whom all blessings flow;
praise him all creatures here below...

We do not yet see this. We call on all creatures world-wide to praise our God, but this is not occurring at the

---

1   Derek Kidner, *Psalms 1-72* (London: Inter-Varsity, 1973), 125.

moment. This will be a 'last thing' affair (cf. Phil. 2:10-11) – it will be but it is 'not yet'. But then the Doxology moves on:

> praise him above, ye heavenly hosts....

There it is – we are caught talking to angels right in church! That, I'm pretty sure, takes place right away, as soon as we ask them to add their deafening adoration to our often meagre efforts. Then the searchlight comes round to us: if we are ordering angels to praise, are we ourselves gripped with the urgency, necessity, and delightfulness of Yahweh's praise?

One of the arenas in which we can see Yahweh's 'glory', the evidence of His goodness, is in the storm. So in verses 3-9 David moves on to say we should be **taking in Yahweh's display on earth**. Here the psalm relates the video and audio of a massive thunderstorm (v. 3) apparently moving off the Mediterranean, working its way eastward and to the north of Israel. The storm breaks cedars: 'Yahweh shattered the cedars of Lebanon.' That's quite impressive, considering those cedars grew to a height of 70-80 feet and that their trunks could sometimes be 30-40 feet in circumference.[2] Even mountains are fragile before Yahweh's storm. When Lebanon and Sirion [=Hermon] are skipping around 'like the young of a wild ox', is it because of the fury of the storm or has an

---

2   J. I. Packer, M. C. Tenney, and William White, eds., *The Bible Almanac* (Nashville: Thomas Nelson, 1980), 255-56.

earthquake been thrown into the mix?[3] Then come the slashes and bolts of lightning, the 'flames of fire' (v. 7) that Yahweh hews out. The storm moves on and convulses wilderness areas (v. 8),[4] thunderous outbursts scaring the female deer into labor and leaving forests in tatters (v. 9). A conservationist's worst nightmare.

This is quite a collage. It's as if David says, Look at what mighty items His voice destroys (v. 5), what massive items He moves (v. 6), what isolated areas He shakes (v. 8), and what a range of creation He affects from the timid doe (v. 9a) to whole forests (v. 9b). And all those 'sons of God' in the heavenly temple explode with 'Glory!' (v. 9c).

We should pause to say that sometimes you may hear the claim that Psalm 29 is really an old Canaanite hymn praising Baal, the storm god, the god of the lightning bolt, and so on, and that biblical writers may have taken it over or adapted it to praise Yahweh. I doubt it. Biblical writers had sufficient theological sophistication that they had no need for Canaanite ghost-writers to express their theology for them. But I don't doubt that Psalm 29 may have Baal theology in view. Not to endorse or imitate but to oppose. Psalm 29 may partly function as 'put-down' theology, as if to say to the pagan media: 'Nuts! Baal is no storm god. Yahweh is God of the storm. Here's a clip

---

3   As Allen Ross suggests (*A Commentary on the Psalms: Volume 1 (1-41)*, Kregel Exegetical Library [Grand Rapids: Kregel, 2011], 659).

4   There is debate about the Kadesh of v. 8b. Some suppose it may refer to Kadesh-barnea of the southern border of Israel, but it could well be the Kadesh about 75 miles north of Damascus on the Orontes River – and so still in the north.

of Him at work. And He brings his storm right across Phoenicia, supposedly Baal's backyard!'

Some people probably wince at the idea of biblical faith using put-downs – it seems rather nasty. But put-downs (well, we can clean them up and call them polemics) are sometimes necessary and very effective. In 1910 President Taft appointed former President Theodore Roosevelt to represent the United States at the funeral of Edward VII. After the funeral the German Kaiser told TR to call on him 'at two o'clock; I have just 45 minutes to give you.' Roosevelt shot back, 'I will be there at two, your Majesty, but, unfortunately, I have but 20 minutes to give you.'[5] That was a put-down and probably an effective one in the face of Teutonic arrogance. So don't lose sleep over the way the Bible may slam Baal worship.

But why does David paint this scenario of 'Yahweh's voice'? Because he wants me to be impressed with Yahweh's glory and majesty. And where might you and I see that 'glory'? We are predisposed to look for it in the full-color placid Vermont farmstead covered in ten inches of pristine snow that appears on the cover of our January devotional booklet. But Psalm 29 implies you might do better watching a Weather Channel re-run of the Six Worst Storms of the Decade. We *say* we agree with this in our hymns but perhaps without much conviction. We have all too little memory of singing:

---

5   Paul F. Boller, Jr., *Presidential Anecdotes* (New York: Penguin, 1982), 210.

His chariots of wrath the deep thunderclouds form,
and dark is his path on the wings of the storm.[6]

Or:

... and clouds arise and tempests blow
    by order from your throne.[7]

Maybe sometimes we're not looking in the right places. When we see Yahweh's storm pounding and pummeling His world, perhaps our first response should be 'Glory!'

Finally, at the end of the psalm, David wants us to be **resting in Yahweh's adequacy for His people** (vv. 10-11). In these two verses David gives us a double revelation of Yahweh, as both reigning King (v. 10) and sustaining God (v. 11).

In verse 10 we meet something of the dual nature of Yahweh's kingship. The first line mentions the flood, *mabbûl*, the word always used of what we call Noah's flood (Gen. 6–8). Since the reference is to a previous historical event, I think the 'perfect' Hebrew verb should be translated as a past tense. Hence: 'Yahweh sat (enthroned) at the flood.' The next line uses the same verb but a different form to point to Yahweh's continuing kingship: 'And Yahweh has seated (himself) as king forever.' So there's a double claim: there is a premier moment of Yahweh's kingship – at the flood, and there is the ongoing exercise of His kingship – forever. (The

---

6   'O Worship the King,' stanza 2.
7   'I Sing the Mighty Power of God,' stanza 3.

earlier episode was not a flash in the pan – His sovereignty continues.)

Why does this matter? Well, we might have a little more put-down theology operating here. In pagan materials like *The Gilgamesh Epic* the gods go berserk over the flood. They 'were terror-stricken at the deluge', 'cowered like dogs and crouched in distress,' and 'Ishtar cried out like a woman in travail'.[8] The gods brought the flood and then were terrified and scared spitless at what they had let loose. But in the Bible we don't have a bunch of divine nervous breakdowns: 'Yahweh [emphatic] sat enthroned at the flood.' He was there. He was in control. He sat as King at the flood, at that supreme chaotic event in the past (v. 10a) and He remains as King forever (v. 10b) – on through whatever His people may face in post-flood time. And that includes times as depicted in verses 3-9 when all seems like chaos in excelsis. Even in that Yahweh reigns.

Now David adds that additional touch: Yahweh is not only reigning King (v. 10) but sustaining God (v. 11):

> Yahweh will give strength to his people;
> Yahweh will bless his people with peace.[9]

We are right back, then, to Psalm 28 (see 28:8)! And, after all the fireworks of verses 3-9, it is fascinating that the last word of the psalm is 'peace'. But we mustn't miss the double emphasis: reigning King, sustaining God. For

---

8   See Alexander Heidel, *The Gilgamesh Epic and Old Testament Parallels* (Chicago: Phoenix, 1963), 85, 249.

9   ESV translates verse 11 as a wish or prayer. I think that is wrong. The subject in both lines ('Yahweh') is emphatic, which seems to go better with a statement than a wish.

though Yahweh is King (v. 10), it's as if He gets down off His throne to put fresh heart into His people.

David McCullough tells about Harry Truman running in a primary election for an eventual US Senate seat. It was 1934 and Missouri was in dire need of rain. On a blistering summer day, near Mexico, Missouri, Truman saw a farmer in a field having trouble with his binder. He stops the car, climbs over the fence, gives a brief introduction, takes off his coat and, as the local paper told it, proceeds 'to set up the binder under a hot sun for his new found friend'.[10] Of course Truman got some political capital out of that but still the deed showed a man who was willing to come into the everyday dilemmas of his fellow citizens. That seems to be the assurance of verse 11 in the context of this psalm. The God whose voice shatters cedars also 'climbs over the fence' to sustain and stabilize His people.

One can hardly study Psalm 29 without conjuring up the episode in Mark 4:35-41. Jesus, asleep in the boat, the storm that even terrified the fishermen among the disciples.... Fully awakened, Jesus rebukes the wind and stifles the sea. Here in the psalm Yahweh brings the storm, in Mark 4 Yahweh calms the storm (cf. v. 41, 'Who then is this?'). Either way He is Lord of the storm. And, anyway, we know that as long as Jesus is in the boat nothing too bad can happen!

---

10   David McCullough, *Truman* (New York: Simon and Schuster, 1992), 209-10.

Psalm 30

A psalm. A song for the dedication of the house. Of David.

(1) I will lift you up, Yahweh,
     for you have drawn me up
     and have not allowed my enemies to rejoice over me.

(2) Yahweh, my God, I cried to you for help
     and you healed me.

(3) Yahweh, you have brought up my life from Sheol;
     you have kept me alive from those going down to the pit.

(4) Sing praise to Yahweh, those he loves,
     and give thanks for the proclamation of his holiness.

(5) For one is in his anger for a moment,
         in his favor for a lifetime;
     weeping may come stay in the evening,
         but at morning a shout of joy!

(6) But I, I had said in my prosperity,
         'I will never, ever be moved.'

(7) Yahweh, in your favor you had made my mountain stand firm;
     you hid your face – I was terrified.

(8) To **you**, Yahweh, I kept crying out,
     and to the Lord I kept pleading for grace:

(9) 'What profit is there in my blood,
   when I go down to the pit?
Will dust give you thanks?
   Will it declare your faithfulness?

(10) Hear, Yahweh, and show grace to me;
O Yahweh, be my helper!'

(11) You have turned my mourning into dancing!
You have loosened my sackcloth and wrapped me in rejoicing!

(12) – That (my) glory may sing praise to you and not be silent;
Yahweh, my God, I will give you thanks for all time!

Evening Weeping, Morning Joy

You may have been through this. You are sorting through old family pictures and here is one of two farmers. Fortunately, your mother or grandmother had written on the back, 'Wayne and Bill in front of machine shop on farm.' Unfortunately, for some, that multiplies uncertainty. The picture is enough of a close-up that it doesn't show much of the machine shop, so you can't tell whether it's Wayne's shop or Bill's. And Bill farmed some rented land six miles west and there was a shop there. So if it was Bill's shop, which one of Bill's shops was this shop? You are sure that you've got Wayne and Bill, but you simply can't nail down the location – there are too many possibilities. That is something like the superscription to Psalm 30. It's a psalm, one of David's. But 'for the dedication of the house' perplexes. Some think it's a song written for the dedication of David's own residence, either early on when he seized Zion (2 Sam. 5:9) or later in a grander structure (2 Sam. 5:11-12). Or, 'house' may mean 'temple'. David, of course, was off the scene by the time Solomon dedicated the temple, but some think of the consecration of the selected *site* for the temple after David's error in numbering the troops (2 Sam. 24:18-25; 1 Chron. 21:18-22:1). Still others suggest the superscription could have been supplied later and may refer to the dedication of the 'second' temple in Ezra 6:13-18, when David's psalm may have been used for the occasion. Such uncertainties, however, do not obliterate the clear message of the psalm: that God's gracious deliverance should stir promiscuous praise. It's a psalm of praise or thanksgiving and yet, not surprisingly, it has a teaching twist. Let's walk our way through it.

First, we hear **the testimony of a desperate man** (vv. 1-3, 11-12). Right away David launches into the immediate urgency of praise. He recounts Yahweh's rescue in terms of *prevention* ('have not allowed my enemies to rejoice over me,' v. 1b); he may not have been under direct attack from enemies, but if David had 'gone under', his enemies would have been thrilled – and Yahweh prevented that. Yahweh's rescue was also a *restoration* ('I cried … and you healed me,' v. 2), but we cannot be sure what kind of restoration it was. 'Healed' could well refer to recovery from literal illness, but it could also be used in a metaphorical sense (cf. 2 Chron. 7:14; Isa. 53:5; 57:18-19; Hos. 14:4). He also speaks of Yahweh's rescue as *preservation:* 'You have brought up my life from Sheol; you have kept me alive from those going down to the pit' (v. 3). Yahweh had kept him from dying. All this immediate praise could well fit God's delivering him from severe illness, yet we must grant that David may be speaking figuratively. In any case, one can scarcely miss the sense of urgency; it's as if David feels under compulsion to jump into praise right away for Yahweh's multi-colored deliverance.

Then, after alluding to other matters in verses 4-10, David comes back to speak of his ongoing debt of praise in verses 11-12. Here he mentions still another aspect of Yahweh's rescue – *transformation*: 'You have turned my mourning into dancing! You have loosened my sackcloth and wrapped me in rejoicing!' (v. 11). God has simply flipped his sadness and grieving on their heads. And with what design? 'That (my) glory may sing praise to you and not be silent' (v. 12a). I think 'my glory' is David's way of referring to himself. David simply says that Yahweh's stellar deliverance was meant to lead him to praise. In fact, continuing praise: 'Yahweh, my God, I will give you thanks for all time!' (v. 12b). True praise remembers – and keeps praising.

Captain Moffatt Burriss was a combat veteran of the European theatre in World War II. In 1993 he fulfilled his desire of going back to visit the battlegrounds of nearly fifty years before. He had been in the so-called Market Garden offensive in Holland. Along with one son and some newly-discovered Dutch friends he went to re-visit the Nijmegen bridge. He saw the grass on the other side of the river, flat ground for 900 yards, where he and others had charged without cover into the face of German artillery, mortars, and machine guns. Later that day his Dutch friends took Burriss and son to see a memorial to the men of the 3rd Battalion, 504th Parachute Infantry

Regiment (Burriss' unit), who were killed in the bridge and river crossing. The names were cast in bronze. Burriss could recall most of them, including voices and faces. There in front of the memorial were several vases of freshly cut flowers. Burris pointed to the flowers and said to his Dutch guides, 'It looks like we came at the right time. What's the occasion?' One of them answered: 'There is no special occasion. Every day, we keep fresh flowers here and at the other memorials. In fact, we bring schoolchildren here regularly so they will know the great price the Americans paid for our freedom.'[1] That's it: there is an ongoing obligation to remember and praise. 'Every day, we keep fresh flowers here.' Hence David's debt. And ours. Not only for various and particular deliverances, but for the deliverance par excellence: 'But you are a chosen generation, a royal priesthood, a holy nation, a people for (God's) possession, so that you might proclaim the mighty acts of the one who called you out of darkness into his marvelous light' (1 Peter 2:9).

Secondly, David tells us of **the tendency of a gracious God** (vv. 4-5). Here the verbs are plural imperatives; he wants to stir up fellow believers to join with him in praise.[2] Verse 5 explains why or for what Yahweh's people should praise Him:

---

1   T. Moffatt Burriss, *Strike and Hold* (Washington, DC: Potomac Books, 2000), 7.

2   He describes the Lord's people as 'those he loves'. The word is *ḥāsîd* (related to *ḥesed* [faithful, unfailing love]), and so refers to those who are the objects of Yahweh's unforsaking love and who, as Alec Motyer would say, love Him back. Another item: verse 4b is a bit difficult. 'Proclamation' is my rendering of *zēker*

For one is in his anger for a moment,
in his favor for a lifetime;
weeping may come stay in the evening,
    but at morning a shout of joy!

He contrasts the tenure of Yahweh's anger and favor. His severity and chastening are fleeting ('for a moment') while His favor is lifelong. Then the next lines depict how this seems to work out in the experience of God's people: weeping may be an overnight guest, but morning brings a shout of joy. He's telling us that God radically changes our circumstances and that, on the whole, His severity and our distress are temporary episodes. He is telling us what is *typical* of God's ways.

Knowing tendencies can be important, or at least useful. I remember as a lad having to ask parental permission to go off and play with a neighborhood chum. If I asked my mother, she might permit me to go down to Tom's place but only for a half-hour, or something of that ilk. Whoopee! My mother had a sort of suspicious nature (somewhat justifiable) and always seemed restrictive even when granting permission. But, if I had my choice, I would always ask my father – 'Can I go across and play at Eddie Phipps' place?' His answer was likely to be, 'Oh, I suppose so,' and he might add, 'Be sure to be home for supper.'

(often 'remembrance', 'memorial'). Some link this term to its use in reference to Yahweh's name (Exod. 3:15) and so translate 'Praise his holy name'. But it can also connote proclamation of God's mighty acts (*NIDOTTE*, 1:1104-5; K-B, 1:271; W. A. VanGemeren, 'Psalms,' EBC, rev. ed., 13 vols. [Grand Rapids: Zondervan, 2008], 5:299). NJB has somewhat paraphrased: 'praise his unforgettable holiness.'

Now my father wasn't a 'permissive' parent; in fact, he ran a pretty tight ship. But in such 'kid' matters, his attitude seemed to be that if something wasn't positively sinful or dangerous there was no harm in it. So, if I was hoping to do something, I would go to my father rather than my mother precisely because I knew his *tendency*. It was the way he was, and, within the confines of my kid-world, it was a heartening encouragement to me.

David then says we should give thanks for Yahweh's tendencies. Not that some troubles are not long-lasting; not that His chastening can't go on for months. But, by and large, so many of our trials are temporary, and the tears that wet our pillow the night before are gone at daybreak. Such turnarounds ought to be fodder for praise.

Third, David recounts for us **the experience of a faltering servant** (vv. 6-10). In these verses David takes us back behind his praise (vv. 1-3) to recall how his trouble had arisen. He gives us, especially in verses 6-7, a flashback and speaks of the arrogance that God must destroy. In verse 6 he confesses his grievous error:

> But I, I had said in my prosperity,
>   'I will never, ever be moved.'

That quote expresses David's attitude (or what he came to see had been his attitude) and then in verse 7a he explains why he had come to have such an outlook: 'Yahweh, in your favor you had made my mountain stand firm.' It was Yahweh's own provision that had given David that sense of security, but somehow (as many of us know) there is a subtle chemistry that corrupts Yahweh's grace into self-sufficiency, that enjoys His goodness and twists it into a self-assured cockiness rather than a God-derived confidence.

There's something despicable about arrogance in any form, let alone in one of God's servants. In 1945 the 'big three', Churchill, Stalin, and Franklin Roosevelt, met at Yalta to talk about the shape of the post-war world. At some point Roosevelt went so far as to tell Churchill: 'I think I can personally handle Stalin better than either your Foreign Office or my State Department.'[3] Utterly arrogant, hopelessly naïve, and eastern Europeans would suffer for decades because, contrary to FDR's expectations, Stalin had handled Roosevelt.

But the Lord can easily dissolve arrogance in one of His own. David tells how in verse 7b: 'You hid your face.' Yahweh in some way removed the light of His presence. David had the only proper reaction: 'I was terrified.'[4]

How does he come out of this darkness? This leads us into verses 8-10 where he relates the argument God hears. Note how he responded to the loss of Yahweh's presence:

> To **you**, Yahweh, I kept crying out,
> and to the Lord I kept pleading for grace (v. 8).[5]

---

3   Larry Schweikart and Michael Allen, *A Patriot's History of the United States* (New York: Sentinel, 2004), 619.

4   Some translations render it 'dismayed', which is too colorless and tame. The word is 'terrified' (*bāhal*).

5   I think the ESV has got it wrong in verse 8; it translates the verbs as present tenses. David is rehearsing what he had done back in his desperate situation.

This is very instructive. When Yahweh hides His face (v. 7b), the only thing to do is to seek His face (v. 8). He does not hide Himself so that we will despair but so that we will seek again and find him.

In verses 9-10 David relates what he said as he was 'pleading for grace'. His initial words may sound strange to us:

What profit is there in my blood,
    when I go down to the pit?
Will dust give you thanks?
    Will it declare your faithfulness? (v. 9).

Surprising words; not exactly what we're accustomed to hear in prayer. But sometimes the surprising is refreshing. I recall reading somewhere of one of those routine airline announcements. Except this one was Kulula Airlines. The voice said: 'Welcome aboard Kulula 271 to Port Elizabeth. To operate your seat belt, insert the metal tab into the buckle, and pull tight. It works just like every other seat belt; and, if you don't know how to operate one, you probably shouldn't be out in public unsupervised.' That gets your attention. You don't expect to hear something like that in a usually tedious and legally-required announcement.

That's the way with David's prayer in verse 9. Who prays like this? Well, David does. What does he mean? He's asking Yahweh what advantage it can possibly be to Yahweh Himself if David dies. If he returns to dust, will that dust give God thanks? Can his corpse rehearse God's faithfulness? He is saying that dead people don't belt out

'Praise, My Soul, the King of Heaven' in the congregation. It's as if he said, 'If I'm dead, I can't sing "'I Greet Thee, Who My Sure Redeemer Art.'" In short: 'If you don't rescue me, you will end up in a praise deficit.' You may recoil from such prayer. But before you do, consider that (1) this prayer 'starts from God's interests,' asking the question, What glory will God have from this?,[6] and (2) it assumes that our whole rationale for existence is to offer praise to God. That in itself is a notch or two above the spirituality of most of us.

---

6   Derek Kidner, *Psalms 1-72* (London: Inter-Varsity, 1973), 129.

Psalm 31

For the music leader. A psalm of David.

(1) In you, Yahweh, I have taken refuge;
     don't ever let me be ashamed;
     in your righteousness let me escape.

(2) Turn your ear to me;
     deliver me quickly;
     be for me a rock of refuge,
       a bastion of fortresses,
       to save me.

(3) For you are my rock and my fortress,
       and on account of your name
       may you lead me and guide me,

(4)   may you bring me out from the net
         which they have hidden for me,
         for you are my refuge.

(5) Into your hand I commit my spirit;
       you have redeemed me, Yahweh, God of truth.

(6) I hate those holding on to empty lies,
     but I, I have trusted in Yahweh.

(7)   I will rejoice and be glad in your faithful love,
          because you have looked on my affliction,
          you have known the distresses of my soul,

(8)   and you have not shut me up in the hand of the enemy;
          you have made my feet stand in a broad place.

(9)   Show grace to me, Yahweh,
          for distress (has come) to me;
          my eye has wasted away because of anguish,
          my soul and my body (as well).

(10) For my life has been finished off with grief
          and my years with groaning;
          my strength fails because of my iniquity
          and my bones waste away.

(11) Because of all my adversaries I have become something
          to mock at,
          –all the more so to my neighbors
          and something to dread to my friends;
          those who see me in the street
              flee from me in horror.

(12) I am forgotten from mind, like a dead person;
          I have become like something that's perishing.

(13) Indeed, I have heard the whispering of many:
          'Terror on every side!'
          (That's) when they huddle up against me
          –they scheme to take my life.

(14) But I, I have trusted in you, Yahweh;
          I have said, 'You are my God.'

(15) My times are in your hand;
          deliver me from the hand of my enemies and my pursuers.

(16) Make your face shine upon your servant,
          save me in your faithful love.

(17) O Yahweh, don't let me be ashamed,
     for I have called upon you;
  let the wicked be ashamed,
     let them be silent (down) in Sheol.

(18) Let lying lips be silent,
  those speaking arrogantly against the righteous
     with pride and contempt.

(19) How massive your goodness which you have stashed away
     for those who fear you,
  (which) you have worked out for those taking refuge in you
     before the sons of men!

(20) You hide them away in the hiding-place of your presence
     from the conspiracies of man;
  you stash them away in a shelter
     from the accusations of tongues.

(21) How blessed Yahweh!
  For he has marvelously demonstrated his faithful love to me
     in a city under siege.

(22) But I, I said in my panic,
     'I have been cut off from before your eyes.'
  But in fact you heard the voice of my pleas for grace
     when I cried to you for help.

(23) Love Yahweh, all his favored ones!
  Yahweh preserves the faithful,
     but abundantly rewards the one acting in pride.

(24) Be strong and let your heart be bold,
  all who are hoping in Yahweh.

In Your Hand

I recall a 'Peanuts' cartoon in which Lucy is trying to pin down the specific malady of another Peanuts character. At last she asks if the person suffers from 'pantophobia', fear of everything, and is assured that she has nailed the problem. Psalm 31 seems a bit like that. That is, it does not appear confined to one theme or focus but takes in several. Part of it seems to be a declaration of faith more than anything else (vv. 1-8), part a description of severe distress (vv. 9-13), some of it an exclamation of thanksgiving (vv. 19-21). We seem to be looking at a collage of the singer's experience rather than at a single, precise situation. But, with a little help from John Newton, perhaps we can summarize the overall message of Psalm 31: *The Lord can be trusted to preserve His servants through many dangers, toils, and snares – and disasters, troubles, fears, and aggravations and assaults.* That about catches it. Our main heads will try to capture how David would describe his various circumstances.

First of all, in verses 1-8 he speaks of **the position I enjoy**. Well, I think he does. There are some who think David goes through his situation from anguish-to-assurance twice in this psalm (vv. 1-8, 9-24; e.g., Kidner). But I'm not convinced of this 'double-take' view. Verses 1-8 are weighted more toward confidence than anguish. Not that there isn't need (vv. 1b, 2a, 4), not that David doesn't appeal (vv. 1b, 2, 4), but Yahweh has dealt adequately with him so that there is a tone of confidence even in the shadow of trouble.

He rests in *God's protection* (vv. 1-4). He claims he has 'taken refuge' in Yahweh (v. 1a); he implies that because Yahweh is eager for righteousness to be done, He will grant him escape (v. 1c); he pleads for Yahweh to be a rock and fortress (v. 2b) but then says that He is precisely that (v. 3a); and he asks for escape from hidden danger because Yahweh already is his refuge (v. 4b). Because Yahweh is all this, his appeal shimmers with expectancy.

Then he also places himself in God's hand, at least partly because he is convinced of *God's reality* (vv. 5-6).[1] 'God of truth' (v. 5b) can be rendered 'faithful God' (as in ESV and NLT), but I have retained 'God of truth' because there seems to be an implicit contrast with the 'empty lies', the no-gods of verse 6a. In Yahweh he trusts in a real God who has really redeemed (likely in past experiences) and whose hand really holds his life. And having Him means he can also revel in *God's compassion* (v. 7), for Yahweh is no stand-offish deity, 'because you have looked on my

---

1   Remember Jesus' use of verse 5a in Luke 23:46, but also remember that it is not an expression of despair but of confidence in a God who redeems.

affliction, you have known the distresses of my soul.' The God of Exodus 3:7 is still being Himself! Nothing distant or clinical about Yahweh; He is always willing to get His hands dirty with my troubles.

In verse 8 David breathes his thanks for what we could call the gift of *God's stability*: far from handing him over to the enemy, 'you have made my feet stand in a broad place' (v. 8b). No tenuous precipices or slippery slopes but plenty of room where one can stand or walk without mishap.

I suggest that in these first eight verses David is saying something like this: 'I am among difficulties and these may become severe, but *this is what I have*; these are the supports God has already given me. All this is nothing to sneeze at.' And naturally that is one way of encouraging himself.

All this conjures up a scenario from college days and following. My father was a pastor, but he had a fixation on automobiles – not 'snooty' ones like Audi or BMWs but Chevvies and Fords and that ilk. When he was in his sixties he underwent a 'conversion' from Chevrolet to Dodge (my brother worked for Chrysler Corporation). He bought a 1964 Dodge Dart, hardly an imposing specimen, but a fairly snappy vehicle with its 'slant six' engine. At various and sundry times Pop would rehearse the virtues of his new vehicle. These mini-lectures were delivered as he was pacing the living room, one hand in pocket, the other slicing the air for emphasis. If I were sitting there, my part was simply to listen and occasionally grunt approval. He would lavish praise on his Dodge – the pick-up it had, its very adequate power on the river hills all around us, and, properly gesturing, he might add, 'And

I don't have to take any slop [his word] off these bigger cars with V-8s – I can stay right with them!' I heard any number of renditions of 'The Virtues of My Auto'. But you see what he was doing? It was an exercise in self-encouragement. With all the 'points' he was making he was essentially saying: 'Now just look at what I have!' That is what David is doing in verses 1-8: In these needs and troubles, look at what I have; look at the position I enjoy.

David moves on as he speaks of **the distress I face** (vv. 9-13). Here his trouble seems far more intense than his allusions in verses 1-8. Distress can be multi-faceted, and he begins by describing it as *exhaustion* (vv. 9b-10):

> [M]y eye has wasted away because of anguish,
>> my soul and my body (as well).
> For my life has been finished off with grief
>> and my years with groaning;
> my strength fails because of my iniquity
>> and my bones waste away.

He says his 'eye' (v. 9b) and his 'bones' (v. 10d) have 'wasted away'. The verb ($\breve{a}\breve{s}e\breve{s}$) occurs also in Psalm 6:7 with similar import: distress and anguish have devastated him physically. 'Eye' (v.9) can be used figuratively, but his stress on soul and body (v. 9) and bones (v. 10) seem to indicate his trouble has wreaked havoc on his physical and emotional condition. And his 'iniquity' has played its part (v. 10c). Hard to say whether he refers to a particular sin or to his overall sinful condition; much of his trouble is external (see vv. 11, 15), but the traitor within makes its own contribution; in any case, that too saps his vitality and sucks his strength. He is utterly enervated.

It gets worse. There is *isolation* (vv. 11-12). He is not only exhausted physically and emotionally but excluded socially. And not merely by 'adversaries' (v. 11a) – one can at least understand their mockery; but there's the silent treatment from neighbors and friends who seem allergic to any contact with him (v. 11b). He has the status of a corpse (v. 12).

There's still more – the psychological: *intimidation* (v. 13). His enemies conspire to inspire fear, insinuating that terror lies in wait everywhere. They are, in fact, scheming to eliminate him. So, whether by frightening suggestion or by actual conspiracy, his enemies create an atmosphere in which he will inhale nothing but fear.

This is a horrid chunk of distress – blatant, nasty, vicious. It doesn't get much worse. Some time ago Marvin Olasky commemorated comedian Henry Youngman in *World* magazine. He passed on some of Youngman's jokes. One was: 'When I told my doctor I couldn't afford an operation, he offered to touch up my x-rays.' But there is no 'touching up' here in the psalm. David lets his distress show up in its raw and unfiltered form. He takes no short cuts in describing how bad it is. But remember: this description is part of his prayer; it is what is told to God. (You the reader are not the audience; you are merely an eavesdropper.) Here is his trouble in all its severity and sadness, in all its awfulness. Yet how blessed he is that he has the freedom to give a full, unedited description of it to God. What privileged people we are, when Hannah-like, we can pour out our souls before Yahweh (cf. 1 Sam. 1:15).

In the third section of the psalm David rehearses **the resources I have** (vv. 14-20). A section like this may seem like it covers the same ground as verses 1-8; but it really doesn't, for here he goes into fuller detail because he responds to the devastating distress he depicted in verses 9-13. It's a sort of when-everything-falls-apart-what-can-you-do section.

First off, he implies that he can *hold on to God's covenant* (v. 14):

> But I, I have trusted in you, Yahweh;
> I have said, 'You are my God.'

There is a typical turning-point: the emphatic, personal pronoun set right down in face of all the preceding muck – 'But I, I ....' Somehow God makes faith so resilient. Then notice what he says he has said: 'You are my God.' That may not exactly turn your lights on. But it should.

I cannot trace all this out step-by-step. I can only sketch it. But what you must see is that 'You are my God' are *responsive* words. The original words are Yahweh's, who has said to His people, 'I shall maintain my covenant ... to be God to you – and to your seed after you' (Gen. 17:7). What does it mean for Yahweh to say He will 'be God to you'? I have quoted it elsewhere but will do so again, for I know of no exposition that digs it out like Donald Macleod's:

> 'I will be your God.' What does that mean? It means that God is saying to Abraham, 'I will be for you. I will exist for you. I will exercise my God-ness for you. I will be committed to you.' There is no way that can be improved

upon! There is no more glorious promise: not in Romans, not in Hebrews, not in Revelation, not in the Gospel of John, not in the Upper Room: nowhere! These words of the Abrahamic covenant have never been excelled and never will.[2]

That's what is packed into 'I will be your God.' But it is only because Yahweh says to us, 'I will be your God,' that we can say, 'You are my God.' It's like 1 John 4:19 – 'We love, because he first loved us.' So we say because He first said to us. 'You are my God' are responsive words in which we say the 'Yes' to Yahweh's 'I will be God to you'.[3] And so here in the terror and darkness of Psalm 31, David is holding on to Yahweh's pledge.

Next, David claims he can *rest in God's hand:* 'My times are in your hand' (v. 15a). Theologically, I suppose we'd say David is trusting God's providence, but there's something more satisfying about keeping the imagery of the biblical text. When he speaks of 'times', he doesn't mean merely his life-span but all the kaleidoscope of circumstances that meet him left and right. Calvin rightly draws attention to the plural form – 'times', and says that David uses it to 'mark the variety of casualties by which the life of man is usually harassed'. That includes *this time* depicted in verses 9-13. But note that 'My times are in your hand' is no placid, anemic bit of resignation. No sooner does he say

---

2   Donald Macleod, *A Faith to Live By*, enl. ed. (Ross-shire: Christian Focus, 2002), 251.

3   '"Thou art my God," has more sweetness in it than any other utterance which human speech can frame' (C. H. Spurgeon, *The Treasury of David*, 7 vols. [London: Passmore and Alabaster, 1876], 2:68).

these words, but he cries, 'Deliver me from the hand of my enemies and my pursuers' (v. 15b). Precisely because my times are in your hand, let that hand deliver me from the hand of my enemies!

How often the truth of this text has proven a bastion and bulwark for God's servants. Ulrich Zwingli, reformer in Zurich, was visiting his people, trying to console sick and dying. The plague had come to Zurich in August 1519. By autumn Zwingli himself had succumbed to the disease. Confined to bed and staring death in the face, Zwingli prayed: 'Do as you will, for I lack nothing. I am your vessel to be restored or destroyed.'[4] Different words, to be sure, but actually just a paraphrase of 'My times are in your hand'. One can rest there even in the plague.

David further implies that he can *expect God's grace:* 'Make your face shine upon your servant, save me in your faithful love' (v. 16). The first of the verse picks up part of the priestly benediction from Numbers 6:25, 'May Yahweh make his face shine toward you, and show grace to you.' This was part of the standard blessing that the priests were to pronounce over Israel, even during Israel's days in the wilderness when she so obviously needed to be 'kept' (Num. 6:24). Doubtless David had heard this benediction often at the sanctuary, and now, in the thick of trouble, he asks Yahweh to activate it in his case, to let His smile be upon him and 'show grace' to him by saving him in his current distress. Isn't that sometimes the way God puts fresh heart into us as well? He takes some semi-

---

4   John D. Woodbridge and Frank A. James III, *Church History Volume Two: From Pre-reformation to the Present Day* (Grand Rapids: Zondervan, 2013), 152.

standard item used in public worship to give us a fresh
view of His goodness. Maybe it's just a clip from a familiar
hymn, 'In every change he faithful will remain,' or, maybe
a pastor's benediction from Psalm 28: 'May the Lord, who
is the strength of his people, be your shepherd and carry
you – forever.' Sometimes it can be something from the
sanctuary that fortifies us for the darkness.

David can also *plead for God's justice* – he not only can
but does beg for it (vv. 17-18):

> Yahweh ... let the wicked be ashamed,
>   let them be silent (down) in Sheol.
> Let lying lips be silent,
> those speaking arrogantly against the righteous
>   with pride and contempt.

One premier problem with the wicked is that they *talk*.
True, they can act and inflict harm, but here David's
focus is not so much on what they do as what they say. If,
however, they are in the grave, that will shut them up,
and that's what David asks for (v. 17b). Sheol has a way
of stifling all their mocking, accusations, threats, and
verbal 'struttery' (v. 18). Some Christians, who may style
themselves as kinder than biblical pray-ers, likely blanch
at what seems such a harsh petition. But I vote for David.
How can Yahweh's servants ever have definitive relief
unless the wicked are decisively muzzled?

Then in verses 19-20 David claims that he can *revel in
God's riches*. Perhaps it would be more appropriate to take
these verses with what follows, but I prefer to keep them
in this segment (vv. 14-20) in which David is tallying up
the 'resources' he has in Yahweh. So he begins (v. 19a)

by erupting in an exclamation of adoration. He delights in Yahweh's goodness, which, he says, 'You have stashed away for those who fear you,' as if Yahweh squirrels away stockpiles of His goodness in hidden storage sites. But the goodness doesn't remain there – Yahweh 'works it out' for those who take refuge in Him (v. 19b). So it is 'stashed away' in His reserve (v. 19a) but then 'worked out' in our experience (v. 19b) where it becomes visible. And the primary form of this goodness seems to be protection from 'the craft and malice' (Alexander) of those who scheme against and accuse Yahweh's people (v. 20). But in the main we should let David's opening salvo percolate in our minds: 'How massive your goodness which you have stashed away for those who fear you!' Do you catch the implication? He is speaking of God's surprises. He is saying that Yahweh has secret treasures of goodness that you are not even aware of, hidden away, ready to use in your behalf. Treasures, we might say, we know nothing about and have never imagined (though Jesus was well aware of them – Matthew 26:53). Hence in our troubles we can, like David, enumerate our resources, like God's covenant or His justice, but there's lots more – His secret riches waiting to be put on display.

We've spent a good bit of paper going through the resources God's servants have (vv. 14-20) in the face of their severe distress (vv. 9-13). The overall impression we should have is that we are not left impoverished even in our worst troubles. Provisions are in place.

Years back the *Daily Bread* devotional booklet passed on a fascinating story. During World War II a farmer in Sussex, England, sent some money to the Scripture Gift

Mission, semi-apologizing that it was not more, but he said the harvest on his farm had been disappointing due to a lack of water. He also mentioned that he was very fearful because the Germans were dropping so many bombs and asked for the mission staff's prayers that he and his family might be spared. One staff member replied that although they couldn't ask the Lord that no bombs would fall on his land (perhaps that was *too* specific?), they would pray that 'God's will in the matter would prevail'. Not long after the farmer had received their reply, a huge German missile crashed down on his place. No family members or livestock were injured. However, the bomb went so deep into the ground that it liberated a submerged stream. The spring kept flowing and provided irrigation not only for our farmer's farm but for those of his neighbors. The next year there was a larger donation!

That's a picture of the psalm situation, especially of the way we have resources in place (vv. 14-20) in the face of the bleakest times (vv. 9-13). And some of those provisions may be 'stashed away', secret affairs that could even have the shape of a German bomb.

Finally, David so much as says, here is **the testimony I bear** (vv. 21-24). This testimony breaks into two parts: first, *of* the Lord's goodness (vv. 21-22), and then, *to* the Lord's people (vv. 23-24). He makes a point to confess his own panic (v. 22) even as Yahweh was at work in his behalf. He holds no inflated view of his own faith. Then on the strength of Yahweh's intervention in his own case, he seeks to hearten Yahweh's people (vv. 23b-24). And yet with that encouragement he includes a 'demand', a necessary response they must make: 'Love Yahweh, all his favored ones' (v. 23a). It's as if he says, 'If you have the kind of God Yahweh has shown Himself to be in my case, what must you do with Him?' Loving Yahweh is the basic response His covenant requires (Deut. 10:12-13); it is ground-level first-commandment stuff. And it's more significant than we customarily imagine.

Donald Grey Barnhouse told of once speaking with a girl at one of the airline desks in the Imperial Hotel in Tokyo. She spoke Chinese, Japanese, and English; she obviously came from a cultured background. Barnhouse asked her if she was a Christian. She told him she was a Buddhist. He inquired a bit further and discovered she had heard of Jesus and knew there was a sacred book, the Bible. But she'd never read it and knew nothing of Christian truth. Then Barnhouse asked her, 'Do you love Buddha?' The very idea astounded her. 'Love? I never thought about love in connection with religion.' Barnhouse went on with a brief explanation of why Christians love the Lord Jesus.[5] And this sort of question is perhaps what we readers of Psalm 31 need. It's not merely a matter of working our way through a psalm under the discipline of a four-point outline and thinking that perhaps I now can see how the psalm fits together. There must be no such detachment. Rather, the psalm shows you what Yahweh is like and how He works, and at the end of it all turns on you and asks, Barnhouse-like, 'Do you *love* Yahweh?'

---

5   Donald Grey Barnhouse, *Let Me Illustrate* (Westwood, NJ: Revell, 1967), 163-64.

Psalm 32

Of David. A maskil.

(1)   How blessed the one whose rebellion is forgiven,
       whose sin is covered!

(2)   How blessed the man whom Yahweh will not charge
       with iniquity,
       the man who has no deceit in his spirit.

(3)   When I kept silent, my bones wore out
       because of my roaring all day long.

(4)   For day and night your hand was heavy upon me;
       my vitality was changed into the droughts of summer. Selah.

(5)   My sin I wanted to acknowledge to you,
       and my iniquity I did not hide;
       I said, 'I will confess my rebellions to Yahweh,'
          – and **you**, you forgave the guilt of my sin! Selah.

(6)   For this let every covenant one pray to you
       at a time when you may be found;
       surely in the deluge of many waters,
          they will never reach him.

(7)   You are a hiding-place for me;
       from distress you preserve me;
       with shouts of deliverance you surround me. Selah.

(8)   I want to give you insight,
       and I want to instruct you in the way you should go,
       I want to counsel you with my eye upon you:

(9)   Don't be like a horse, like a mule,
             that have no sense;
         bridle and bit are its trappings to restrain it,
             (or) it won't come near you.

(10) The pains of the wicked are many;
        but the one trusting in Yahweh
            – covenant love wraps around him!

(11) Be glad in Yahweh and rejoice, O righteous ones!
        And shout for joy, you who are upright in heart!

How Do You Spell 'Relief'?

Some years back there was a toothpaste called Gleem. I think it's still obtainable but not nearly so popular as it once was. Apparently advertising investigators had discovered that many of the tooth-bearing populace felt vaguely guilty because they didn't brush their teeth after every meal. So Gleem pitched its dental gospel to these people by telling them it was designed for folks who 'can't brush their teeth after every meal'.[1] Dentifrice absolution.

Naturally when we are not bewitched by the gimmicks of advertising, we know that toothpaste guilt is not real guilt but false guilt. However, our contemporary culture places much guilt in the 'false guilt' category. Someone has guilt feelings which he feels he shouldn't feel and so seeks some recourse to eliminate them. Not that there isn't false

---

1   Vance Packard, *The Hidden Persuaders* (New York: Pocket Cardinal, 1958), 58.

guilt, but there's truly something wrong when most guilt is assumed to be false guilt. Which is why it's so refreshing to get shoved in among Christ's church – it's so counter-cultural. As someone has said, only the church engages in confession of sin.[2] The Rotary Club doesn't mess with the confession of sins, nor does the United States Congress, nor the National Association of Okra and Cauliflower Growers, but if you creep into a church, you're likely to hear people confessing their sins.

Now David is our teacher in this matter in Psalm 32. He endured a devastating bout with guilt. Some think Psalm 32 comes out of the same background as Psalm 51, the Uriah-Bathsheba affair (see 2 Sam. 11-12). But we don't know; we can't be sure. Better not to worry about it and move on to ask what Psalm 32 teaches. We might sum it up under three heads.

The first is: **the misery of guilt and the mercy of misery** (vv. 3-4). Verses 1-2 form a 'conclusion' that is stated first, but verses 3-4 recount the experience that preceded that conclusion.[3]

David depicts his misery – it came in the wake of his keeping 'silent'. The time of silence was the time of unconfessed sin, and he says it was *wearing* (v. 3, 'my bones wore out'), *weighty* (v. 4a, 'day and night your hand was heavy upon me'), and *withering* (v. 4b, 'my vitality was

---

2   I realize quite a number of churches do not. They are so taken with singing for 35 minutes at a stretch (or watching performers sing) that little or no time is left in their services for prayer, let alone prayers of confession.

3   Psalm 73 is like this. Verse 1 states the position Asaph came to after his nasty ordeal noted in verses 2-12 (or 2-17).

changed into the droughts of summer'). So, among other things, David endured ongoing insomnia (v. 4a), draining fatigue (v. 4b), and general exhaustion (v. 3), what we might call psychosomatic effects of unconfessed sin. David gives us a picture of the destructiveness of guilt.[4] We're not claiming that unconfessed guilt is always the root of such troubles, but it can sometimes be the root cause. Sometimes it can be that simple.

Once in his later years Boston Red Sox baseball legend, Ted Williams, was back visiting in the Red Sox front office. He was told he ought to go by and say hello to Helen Robinson, who was the team's legendary telephone operator. Her work tenure had extended back into Williams' playing days. She was delighted to see Ted and told him to 'come over here and I'll give you a hug'. That was done but a Red Sox executive standing near noticed tears streaming down Helen's cheek. He later asked Helen why she had been crying and the mystery dissolved. 'He was standing on my foot. I knew he couldn't see well, and I didn't have the heart to tell him to get off.'[5] He was standing on her foot. It was that simple. And sometimes the misery of mind and body can be because of unconfessed sin. It can be that simple.

But, David says, there is mercy in and with the misery. 'Day and night your hand was heavy upon me.' The misery was miserable, but God was at work in it. Yahweh Himself was mixed up in this misery, indeed causing it, or at least aggravating it. The misery of sin can be a gift from God.

---

4   Cf., the instance Martyn Lloyd-Jones cites in *Healing and the Scriptures* (Nashville: Oliver-Nelson, 1988), 150-52.

5   Ben Bradlee, Jr., *The Kid* (New York: Little, Brown, 2013), 683.

It is divine pressure meant to drive us to confession and forgiveness. Sometimes extreme methods must be used. Rev. Walter Ross was licensed to preach in 1714 but found the folks around Kilmuir (Scotland) unruly and rather barbaric. One village kept active watch for his approach. One day the alarm was spread that he was coming, and the people vamoosed from their homes, got into their boats and sailed out some distance from shore. Mr. Ross was angry when finding the homes empty, so he went into a number of the houses, relieved them of cooking implements, and locked up the latter in a safe place. Eventually hunger forced the locals to meet with Ross, but he had to use severe measures to bring that about.[6]

So the Lord may prey on your conscience, day and night, if need be. He may not flinch to use the most extreme and painful measures. God is so good to you that He refuses to allow you to be comfortable and happy in sin. There is mercy in the misery.

Secondly, we must notice **the anatomy of sin and the vocabulary of forgiveness** (vv. 1-2, 5). Verses 1-2 strike a tone of ecstasy, but we are not quite there yet. Let's stop first to dwell on some of the sin-words David uses.

'Rebellion' (*peša'*), sometimes rendered 'transgression', is refusing subjection to rightful authority, in this case to Yahweh, the legitimate king, and to His covenant Law. The related verb can be used of political revolt or rebellion (2 Kings 1:1). There is an attitude that lurks beneath the

---

6   Tom Lennie, *Land of Many Revivals* (Ross-shire: Christian Focus, 2015), 143-44n.

external action. Our maternal grandfather was once babysitting two of my older brothers when they were small. At bedtime he told them it was time for them to get upstairs. My number two brother, maybe three or four at the time, retorted, 'You're not my boss.' So Grandpa Wilson had to show him he was the boss. The story as I have it is that Grandpa whacked Glenn on the backside, and he went up one step. Then another whack and he went up another. And so on until he had completely ascended and realized who the boss was! But that is the attitude of *peša'*.

Then David mentions 'sin'. The word comes from the root *ht'*, which occurs about 600 times in the Old Testament, the commonest root for 'sin'. Though we must not push the matter, it sometimes carries the idea of failure or 'missing' a mark or goal (cf. Judg. 20:16; Prov. 8:36; 19:2).[7] 'Sin' is certainly a coming short of God's intention or requirements. One might think of a very competitive college basketball game. If some player takes a shot that doesn't even hit the rim, those cheering for the opponent may mock him by chanting, 'Air ball! Air ball!' Because it fell short.

Next David mentions 'iniquity' (*'āwōn*). The root may suggest being bent or twisted or being made crooked (cf. Lam. 3:9), and so a perversion or distortion.[8] I always associate this word with a bedrail in our oldest son's bedroom. In their younger days, our boys used to love to imitate professional wrestlers, and they did some of this in

---

7   Cf. *TWOT*, 1:277-78.

8   Cf. *TWOT*, 2:650-51.

Luke's bedroom. I noticed that his bed had sagged on the one side. The problem was that the angle iron of the bedrail had been twisted, wrenched out of its proper shape. It was because of the boys' jumping on and 'hammering' each other on that bed. I tried the sledgehammer to whack it back into shape, but it was useless; I had to put several bricks under that bedrail to get the bed level. It was simply wrung out of shape, hopelessly wrenched and twisted. To a certain extent that is 'iniquity', a perversion of a proper condition.

David's blessing also alludes to 'deceit' (v. 2b). Deceit is at work whenever one denies or hides, extenuates or excuses, this or that favorite sin. It's the engine behind the whole cover-up process.

Verses 1-2 are not meant to give us a detailed picture of sin, not meant to make Anglicans or Presbyterians more familiar with Hebrew words; rather, these verses express the excited joy of forgiveness – but it is a joy you will never know unless you realize that sin is not some semi-naughty act but a multifaceted, complex octopus-like monster that has you. You must see the treason of sin, the failure of sin, the twistedness of sin, the duplicity of sin; you must see that you are in revolt against the only true King, continually missing the mark of what He requires, having a twisted, perverse nature that excels in covering up the cancer – or forgiveness will not mean squat to you.

Now David also speaks of forgiveness here. He speaks of the one whose rebellion is 'forgiven'. The verb is *nāsā'*, a common verb that means to lift up and/or carry away; hence forgiveness is like relief from a burden. Then he alludes to sin being 'covered'. The verb is *kāsâ*. There is a paradox between its use in verse 1b and its use in verse 5. In the latter David said, 'I did not *kāsâ* (cover) my iniquity.' He had done that – see verses 3-4. But when we uncover our sin (v. 5), God covers it (v. 1b); when we cover it (up), it remains uncovered. So forgiveness is like the hiding of a record. Then David speaks of God's 'not charging' one with iniquity (the negative with the verb *ḥāšab*); that is, He does not hold us liable for iniquity, and so depicts forgiveness as the dismissal of a debt. Yahweh meets the anatomy of sin with the vocabulary of forgiveness: it is relief from a burden, the hiding of a record, the dismissal of a debt.

We might tarry a moment in the land of biblical theology and ask, 'How can these things be?' If rebellion is lifted, who carries it? Peter, drawing on Isaiah 53:12, tells us Jesus Himself 'carried our sins in his body upon the tree' (1 Peter 2:24). If sin is covered, how has it happened? 'He erased the certificate of debt ... that was against us ... and has taken it out of the way by nailing it to the cross' (Col. 2:14). If we are not charged with iniquity, who pays? 'But the LORD made the punishment fall on him, the punishment all of us deserved' (Isa. 53:6b, TEV). Jesus carried the load, erased the record, paid the debt.

Yet we must go beyond the vocabulary of forgiveness. Look at verse 5 and the emphasis there:

My sin I wanted to acknowledge to you,
and my iniquity I did not hide;
I said, 'I will confess my rebellions to Yahweh,'
        and **you**, you forgave the guilt of my sin!

I want to draw attention to the emphatic 'you' in the last line, but first I need to touch on this matter of confession. Obviously David is saying that confession was a condition of his forgiveness. However, it's crucial to see that a condition is not a cause. Confession is essential but it does not convey forgiveness. That can only come from the One who has been wronged. Let's say you have gangrene. However, let's say that for weeks and months you have denied it. You have refused to acknowledge that you have gangrene. Then, finally, you admit it. Your 'confession' does nothing to cure your malady. It's a necessary preliminary toward a possible cure but your admission in itself does not effect that.

Beyond his confession, however, David revels in the thrill of forgiveness: 'And **you**, you forgave the guilt of my sin!' Sadly, it's often hard for us to feel David's joy. Part of this may be because we seldom ponder the sheer miracle of God's nature; He has become about as impressive to us as a box of Kellogg's Corn Flakes. How we should shudder to say, 'Who is a God like you –pardoning iniquity and passing over rebellion...' (Micah 7:18). It's almost too much to hope for, almost something that shouldn't happen.

David Redding passes on a story that a prison warden loved to tell. It involved a friend of the warden, who once was on a train and noticed the fellow sitting next to him was very low and woebegone. His young companion confessed that he was a just released convict from a distant penitentiary. His whole life had cast a shadow over his family; his criminal record had heaped shame on them. And he had lost almost all contact with them. He couldn't help hoping against hope, however, that the almost total silence of many years meant that they were too poor maybe or too illiterate to write. So, he said, before his prison sentence was up, he had hatched a plan to find out how they felt – one that would not be too hard for either of them. He wrote a letter home explaining that he would be on this train that passed their little farm on the outskirts of town. If they could forgive him, they were to hang a white ribbon on the old apple tree near the tracks. If it was not hanging there when his train went by, he would never bother them again. As the train approached the familiar haunts of his childhood, the suspense was more than he could take. So he exchanged seats with his companion and asked him to watch and report the result to him. In a minute the tree was in sight; his companion's eyes filled with tears; he placed his hand on the young man's knee and in a hoarse whisper said, 'It's all right. The whole tree is white with ribbons.'[9] Such should be the thrill and relief of Yahweh's forgiveness.

Thirdly, David underscores **the lessons of experience and the call to joy** (vv. 6-11). The lessons come first and the first of those is that you should crave this unhindered fellowship in prayer (vv. 6-7). Verse 6 begins, 'For this let every covenant one pray to you at a time of finding' (literally). I take the 'this' as referring to the enjoyment of that open confession-forgiveness relation noted in verse 5. 'Covenant one' is *ḥāsîd*, the one God loves and who loves Him in return (Motyer). We're not talking here of the wicked and the pagans; but every

---

9   David A. Redding, *The Parables He Told* (New York: Harper & Row, 1976), 50-51.

Yahweh-lover should be eager to seek God in prayer and enjoy a reconciled relation with Him. Besides craving this prayer-fellowship, verses 6b-7 suggest that extra benefits come with it.

I admit the connection is difficult here, but I agree with Alec Motyer that verses 6b-7 (regarding the 'deluge of many waters' and 'distress') indicate that 'by repentance one comes into a new sphere of divine protection amid the storms of life'.[10] With the reconciled relation (vv. 5-6a) comes also a certain security (vv. 6b-7). Not that one is immune but preserved, not that one may not be overtaken but not overwhelmed. The upshot seems to be that the verse-5-kind-of-relation gives an overall stability to a believer's life. I cannot boast of grand experiences with God. I can only say that as a sinner I could not bear existence if I did not know that for Jesus' sake I live under the smile of my Father and in that relation go walking on into sadnesses, disappointments, and troubles, expecting Him to be a hiding-place for me.

The second lesson is that you should be sensitive to God's pressure on your conscience (vv. 8-9). There's a bit of a debate about the 'I' in verse 8, in words like 'I want to instruct you in the way you should go, I want to counsel you with my eye upon you.' Some expositors think God speaks here, probably, in large measure, because it 'sounds' like it. Yet there is no overt indication of a change of speaker, so I take these to be David's words, the instruction he wants to pass on based on his experience.

---

10 Leslie S. M'Caw and J. A. Motyer, 'Psalms,' in *The New Bible Commentary: Revised* (London: Inter-Varsity, 1970), 471.

In verse 9 he goes to the farm, to horses and mules. The trouble is that horses can horse around, and mules can be, well, mule-ish, and they won't do what you want unless you have them under bit and bridle. David's instruction is: Don't be mule-ish.[11] Don't be like I was in verses 3-4; you can avoid the divine pressure-cooker. Why should God have to break you? David gives no details about his specific sin; he simply passes on what he has learned. Have a tender conscience, he says, not a hard heart. Don't be dense about admitting your sin.

Now I know North American baseball does not make sense to all readers; for those in the UK, in more ways than one, baseball is not quite cricket. But this is rather easy. In baseball, coaches have 'signs' they give to a batter as he goes into the batter's box, signs that the other team, hopefully, cannot figure out. A coach may flash a batter a sign that he is to bunt – that is, not to swing hard but to tap the ball into the ground not far from home plate. That batter is usually thrown out, but this procedure often moves another base runner into scoring position. Some years ago a fellow named Zeke Bonura played for the Chicago White Sox. He was a good hitter but rather slow on the uptake, as we say. Sometimes he would be about to enter the batter's box but would stand outside of it, staring uncomprehendingly at his manager who was giving him the 'sign' from the third base coaching box. Once his manager, Jimmy Dykes, flashed Bonura the 'bunt' sign. He didn't 'get' it. Dykes finally became so exasperated

---

11   That is the way G. Douglas Young put it in our OT Poets class at Trinity Evangelical Divinity School.

at Bonura's baffled, muddled puzzlement, that he simply shouted, 'Bunt, you meathead. Bunt. Bunt! B-U-N-T.'[12]

Obviously David never heard of Zeke Bonura. But if he had, he might have said, 'That's what I'm talking about!' But he did know mules, and he clearly *does* say, 'Don't be dense, don't be stubborn, don't be "thick". Don't make it necessary for God to turn up the heat and make you miserable before you will confess your guilt. Have a soft heart toward God's convicting work.'

Then in verses 10-11 David issues his call to joy. He picks up the keynote from verses 1-2 when he began, 'How blessed... how blessed!' So he exclaims, 'Be glad in Yahweh and rejoice, O righteous ones!' (v. 11a). Who are the 'righteous ones'? If we look at the near-by parallels they consist of 'the one trusting in Yahweh' (v. 10b) and those 'who are upright in heart' (v. 11b). But then, more broadly, they are those in verses 1-5 who have been forgiven iniquity and rebellion and sin. So the contrast in verses 10-11 is not between the wicked and the perfect but between the wicked and the 'righteous', that is, the forgiven. And who has more reason for joy than they? This joy oozes out of the first stanza of one of Isaac Watts' communion hymns:[13]

> Jesus invites his saints
> >to meet around His board;

---

12 Daniel Okrent and Steve Wulf, *Baseball Anecdotes* (New York: Oxford, 1989), 149.

13 Can easily be sung to the tune 'Festal Song'. You may access the whole hymn in *Christian Hymns* (Bridgend: Evangelical Movement of Wales, 1977), No. 420.

here pardoned rebels sit and hold
        communion with their Lord.

How do you spell relief? In God's dictionary it begins with
an 'f' – forgiveness. And His people never get over it.

Psalm 33

(1) Shout for joy in Yahweh, you righteous ones
– praise is a beautiful thing for the upright.

(2) Give thanks to Yahweh with the lyre;
on the ten-stringed harp play to him;

(3) sing to him a new song,
play with skill with shouting;

(4) for the word of Yahweh is upright
and all his work is in faithfulness;

(5) he loves righteousness and justice;
the earth is full of Yahweh's unfailing love!

(6) By the word of Yahweh the heavens were made,
and all their host by the breath of his mouth;

(7) he gathers the waters of the sea like a heap;
he places the ocean deeps in storage places;

(8) let all the earth be afraid of Yahweh;
let all the world's residents feel dread of him;

(9) for **he** spoke – and it came to be,
he commanded – and there it stood!

(10) **Yahweh** frustrates the plan of nations;
     he hinders the designs of peoples.

(11) Yahweh's plan will stand forever,
     the design of his heart to generation after generation.

(12) How happy the nation who has Yahweh for its God,
     the people he chose for his own possession!

(13) From heaven Yahweh looks down;
     he sees all the sons of man;

(14) from the place of his dwelling he gazes (down)
          at all earth's residents.

(15) He is the One who forms their hearts, each one,
     the One who discerns all their activities.

(16) No king is saved by a huge army,
     a warrior is not delivered by massive strength;

(17) a horse is an utter disappointment for victory,
     and by its great strength it cannot deliver.

(18) Why, the eye of Yahweh is on those who fear him,
     on those waiting for his unfailing love,

(19) to deliver their life from death
     and to keep them alive in famine.

(20) Our soul waits for Yahweh
     – he is our help and our shield.

(21) Yes, in him our heart will rejoice,
     for we have trusted in his holy name.

(22) Let your unfailing love, Yahweh, rest upon us,
     even as we have waited for you.

Good Reasons

for a New Song

We have friends with whom we occasionally go out to eat. When the husband gives his order, he indicates he wants coffee and then also a glass of milk with his meal. So the initial drinks arrive but by the time the food comes the waitress almost always has forgotten the glass of milk. So he says, 'Milk!' And off she goes. He uses a good bit of cream in his coffee, so when that's depleted, he calls, 'Cream!' Of course, during the meal his coffee runs low, so he barks out, 'Coffee!' If he has a baked potato and the trimmings are deficient, he may call, 'Butter!' He always craves ketchup with his meat, so when the meal is served, his 'Ketchup!' sends her off to secure the missing condiment. My wife and I get amused by these one-word staccato demands, but then we're not the waitress. We are also a bit embarrassed. He may not realize it, but *he never says thanks* when any of these items arrive. I often think that the harried waitress must cringe to come near our table and so, when paying my bill, I always include an extra-generous tip to compensate for her somewhat thankless task.

Psalm 33 assumes that such should never be the case among Yahweh's people – they have all sorts of reasons for thanks and praise (vv. 4-22); even so, the psalmist prefaces those 'reasons' with a call to praise (vv. 1-3) meant to stir them up to their proper task of giving thanks with vocal and musical vigor.[1]

We should underscore a couple of notes in this preface. Derek Kidner has called attention to verse 3 as a superb synopsis of 'three qualities rarely found together in religious music'.[2] There is freshness: 'Sing to him a new song.' A 'new' song implies there are always fresh reasons for praising Yahweh (Alexander) and yet new songs can also remember old acts of God's power and grace that are newly prized (cf. Maclaren). So praise should never be stale. And there is finesse: 'play with skill.' This does not mean our praise must have a professional touch, but it does mean it should not be sloppy. Our praise should operate on the premise that Yahweh's praise deserves our very best effort. And then fervor has a place: 'with shouting.' There ought to be a certain vitality and vigor about our praise, nothing cold or nonchalant. You may remember that story at the end of 2 Samuel 6, of David dancing and

---

1   Note the vocabulary which 32:11 and 33:1 share: 'righteous ones,' 'upright,' 'shout for joy.' This may help explain why the Psalms' editors placed these psalms next each other.

2   *Psalms 1-72* (London: Inter-Varsity, 1973), 136. He goes on to add: 'In due course the quiet close of the psalm will make the further point that jubilance is not the only mood in worship.'

gyrating before the ark of Yahweh as it entered Jerusalem. Perhaps you also recall how his wife Michal went out and chewed David out over his exuberant conduct, telling him how disgusting he was. Whether you lean toward David's joyful exuberance or Michal's rigid propriety, William Blaikie has summed it up well:

> There are, doubtless, times to be calm, and times to be enthusiastic; but can it be right to give all our coldness to Christ and all our enthusiasm to the world?[3]

Verse 3, then, supplies us with the elements we need to combine in a balanced practice of praise.

There's one other matter we should note – that there's an 'aesthetic' aspect to praise. The last of verse 1 says, 'Praise is a beautiful thing for the upright.' Don't we often find it so? I recall one Sunday evening at First Presbyterian Church, Columbia, South Carolina, when we joined to sing a William Gadsby hymn to the tune 'Toulon'. Sometimes one can sense conviction in the way a congregation sings a hymn, and I thought as I both sang and heard, 'This has grabbed them deep down inside,' as they sang:

> Immortal honours rest on Jesus' head,
> my God, my portion, and my living Bread;
> in Him I live, upon Him cast my care;
> He saves from death, destruction, and despair.

---

3   W. G. Blaikie, *The Second Book of Samuel*, The Expositor's Bible (Cincinnati: Jennings & Graham, n.d.), 96.

It wasn't merely the volume with which the congregation sang; it was the sense that people were saying an emphatic 'Yes!' as they sang. And it was 'a beautiful thing'.

Or what can one say when the Lord's people are standing and singing 'Be Still, My Soul,' and perhaps from where one stands one sees a woman recently and sadly and abruptly widowed? But she is singing with the rest of us:

> Be still, my soul: the Lord is on your side;
> bear patiently the cross of grief or pain;
> leave to your God to order and provide;
> in every change he faithful will remain ...

Yes, 'in every change.' And, again, it's 'a beautiful thing'.

That seems like a long introduction. Psalm 33 will get us into the reasons for praise, but before it does so, verses 1-3 'prep' us for the task, tell us how to praise, and how we should look on the whole exercise. Now we are ready to trace the message of Psalm 33, which is that *the people of God have plenty of fuel to ignite their praise*. The rest of the psalm takes us through the reasons we have for praise of Yahweh. Verses 1-3 provide the imperatives ('Shout for joy,' 'give thanks,' 'play,' 'sing,' 'play with skill') and verse 4 with its causal 'for' begins to supply the incentives.

First, we are to praise God for **His work in creation** (vv. 4-9). The writer's first statement is, 'For the word of Yahweh is upright' (v. 4a). That strikes the keynote in this 'creation' segment – three times he stresses the word (or speech) of Yahweh (vv. 4, 6, 9). When he says Yahweh's word is 'upright' or 'straight', it likely means it is uttered in total sincerity with complete intent to bring about that word (cf. Alexander). So His *word* is carried out in His *work* faithfully done (v. 4b).

One could say that verses 4-5 set out the venue for Yahweh's display of His creation work. Note what a collage of terms we have here: upright, faithfulness, righteousness, justice, unfailing love. He will speak of creation but first the writer wants us to see where it comes from: from the massive rightness and goodness of Yahweh's character. He highlights Yahweh's 'bias' in verse 5a: 'he loves righteousness and justice.'[4] You must be clear about *the kind of being* who does this creative work. And then he erupts in that stellar exclamation of verse 5b: 'the earth is full of Yahweh's unfailing love!' That is His *ḥesed*, His covenant love, His love that sticks and stays and refuses to let go.[5]

What is so striking about verse 5b is that you would never catch a pagan saying anything like that. For example, you would never hear a pagan in Mesopotamia saying, 'The earth is full of Marduk's unfailing love!' Or, 'The earth is full of Ishtar's unfailing love!' Unfailing love? Marduk? Ishtar?[6] Are you bananas? Such pagans would never dream of saying such a thing. The whole raft

---

4   Alec Motyer reminds us that when 'they occur together like this, "righteousness" refers to righteous principles and "judgment" [or, justice] to righteous application and practice' (*Psalms by the Day* [Ross-shire: Christian Focus, 2016], 82).

5   Compare Isaiah 6:3, 'His glory is what fills all the earth.' Here in Psalm 33:5, however, the earth is full of Yahweh's *ḥesed* rather than His *kabōd* (glory).

6   Cf. Alexander Heidel, *The Gilgamesh Epic and Old Testament Parallels* (Chicago: U. of Chicago, 1949), 49-52 (Gilgamesh's 'critique' of Ishtar).

of pagan deities was capricious; one could never know what they might do or un-do, and because pagan deities had such an unpredictable character, one could never be sure of anything. They were morally indifferent, and none of them was in final and supreme control (even the gods were subject to a realm beyond them – magic). That's why some scholars have characterized Mesopotamian society as suffering from 'overtones of anxiety'.[7] For the earnest pagan the earth was not full of unfailing love but of constant fear and never-ending uncertainty. Do you realize what you have if you can stand and exclaim verse 5b with the psalmist?

The psalmist moves on to give samples of God's power in creation (vv. 6-8). One comes from what we might call the 'upper' arena (v. 6) and one from the 'lower' (v. 7). He's fascinated by the manner of creation, especially in verse 6:

> By the word of Yahweh the heavens were made,
> and all their host by the breath of his mouth.

He is picking up on the language of Genesis 1: 'Then God said, "Let there be ...," and there was ....' (Gen. 1:3). He remembers how the mere word executed the steps of creation. 'Then God said, "Let there be an expanse in the middle of the waters...," and that's the way it was' (Gen. 1:6-7). Or, 'Then God said, "Let the waters under the sky be gathered to one place...," and that's the way it was' (Gen. 1:9). Verse 6 (of our psalm) wants to underscore the

---

7   See Nahum Sarna, *Understanding Genesis* (New York: Schocken, 1966), 17.

ease and effortlessness of Yahweh's creation; the heavens and their residents were simply the result of Yahweh's mere word, the breath of His mouth. Verse 7 moves beyond creation to preservation and providence. The verb forms in verse 7 are participles, and so seem to refer not merely to Yahweh's 'original' but to His ongoing work:

> He gathers the waters of the sea like a heap;
> he places the ocean deeps in storage places.

It seems to me that in this lower-level picture he wants to stagger us with God's *immensity*. Think of the control He exercises – gathering up the vast and unruly seas in a heap and assigning ocean depths to their respective storage facilities! And a God this mighty and massive should stir a proper response in His world – all the earth should 'be afraid of' Yahweh, all the world's residents should 'feel dread' of Him (v. 8). Please, don't anyone spout nonsense like, 'This doesn't mean we should be afraid, just that we should have reverence.' No, you should be afraid, you should feel dread; it should intimidate you;[8] seeing His work in creation should buckle your knees. And then it may produce reverence; but don't try to bypass the fear and trembling with your canned pastel explanations.

Finally, in verse 9, he comes back to what really ought to stagger us:

> For **he** spoke – and it came to be,
> **he** commanded – and there it stood!

---

8   Allen Ross, *A Commentary on the Psalms: Volume 1 (1-41)*, Kregel Exegetical Library (Grand Rapids: Kregel, 2011), 733.

It's almost as if he said, 'God's creation is really rather simple, you know; He said what He wanted and that's what happened.' As in verse 6, the writer is harking back to Genesis 1 – God said, 'Let there be' and that's the way it was. But this is not merely a word about God's creating power – there is grace in this word for us.

How so? Creation came about by God's *word*. That word is the expression of God's *will*. Therefore each step of creation (cf. Gen. 1) fulfills the design of His personal will. He then specially *intends,* that is, He *wants* each part of His creation to exist. Hence purpose and meaning are in the very warp and woof of God's world. This is light years apart from the Babylonian mythology in which the victorious Marduk takes the defeated goddess Tiamat, hacks her corpse in two, half for the sky and half to make the earth. 'Creation' there is at best a sort of accidental after-thought. There is no purpose bred into the grist of that gross piece of work. But if creation is by God's word, it is then by His will and intention and design, and so there is *purpose* in God's world and that should cast out any ultimate despair for me. It should nix nihilism. This does not mean that God's saints won't have days when they may be utterly downcast; it does not mean they will never *feel* despairing; but if they understand what Psalm 33 (and Genesis 1) implies, it will build a floor in any seemingly bottomless pit.

Secondly, we should praise God for **His work in history** (vv. 10-15). Yahweh does not keep Himself marooned in creation; He messes in politics. He gets into the dirty stuff of history. This is partly what makes the God of the Bible so unnerving – you simply can't box

Him up in one arena of His world. He simply 'takes over' everywhere.

We can break down this chunk of the psalm into sections. The first we can call *frustration and election* (vv. 10-12). Here verses 10-11 go together and yet stand in contrast. Verse 10a tells us that 'Yahweh [emphatic] frustrates the plan of nations,' whereas verse 11a assures that 'Yahweh's plan will stand forever'. 'Plan' comes from a root *yā 'aṣ* that means to counsel, purpose, or plan. So there is the plan of nations and there is Yahweh's plan; Yahweh bungles up the former but always fulfills the latter. Then verse 10b says that Yahweh 'hinders the designs of peoples', while, once more, verse 11b affirms that the 'designs of [Yahweh's] heart' stand up, down through the generations. 'Designs' comes from a root *ḥāšab* that means to think or devise. There is this deliberate contrast between the 'plan' and 'designs' of Yahweh and those of the nations. Yahweh, then, carries out His plan and designs in history, but part of His work in history consists in frustrating and negating the schemes of nations. You may think history is pretty much of a mess, but ponder what it would be like if nations were consistently successful in their schemes. Who knows how many devious plots of nations that Yahweh has nixed before they got off the ground!

I think it wrong to separate verse 12 from verses 10-11. Verse 11 speaks of Yahweh's plan and designs and verse 12 indicates what at least part of that plan is. Verse 12 begins with an exclamation: 'How happy the nation who has Yahweh for its God!' Then the second half of verse 12 defines that 'nation', namely, 'the people he chose for his own possession.' If we want to be picky, they are not those who chose Yahweh and so call Him their God; rather, they are the people Yahweh chose to make His own, and in view of that He is their God. Link this up with verse 11. What is Yahweh's 'plan', or what are His 'designs'? Verse 12 implies: to have a people He chooses to belong to Him in this world. What a high privilege indeed to be a nation and people Yahweh chose for Himself among all the other 'nations' and 'peoples' (v. 10).

If you see many pictures of Winston Churchill, you'll see a good many in which a cigar protrudes from his mouth. Some of his partly-smoked cigars have appeared at auction and have gone for as much as 4,500 pounds.[9] Normally used cigars don't stir our interest, but in this case the difference arose from *whose they were*. That is why this people in verse 12 are so happy and blessed. Not because they are so memorable or impressive in themselves, but because of the One to whom they belong. And so, in what may sometimes seem the mess and muck and menagerie of nations and peoples (v. 10), there stands the church (v. 12). And that church would not be standing there unless – as Psalm 124 insists – Yahweh goes about His international frustrating and hindering work.

We can call the second segment of God's work in history *scrutiny and accountability* (vv. 13-15). Here Yahweh looks down (v. 13a), sees (v. 13b), gazes down (v. 14), discerns (v. 15) – all verbs of perception and insight. Note the repeated use of 'all'/'each': 'all the sons of man' (v. 13), 'all earth's residents' (v. 14), each heart (v. 15a),

---

9   Christopher Catherwood, *Churchill: The Greatest Briton* (London: Sevenoaks, 2018), 100.

'all their activities' (v. 15b). Verse 15 indicates that Yahweh thoroughly knows both the internal (hearts) and external (activities) aspects of man's existence. Why would the psalmist lay such stress on God's extensive and intensive knowledge of all people and each person? Is it not because they will at some point be held accountable for what they are and do? Isn't the implication that Yahweh doesn't only frustrate and hinder nations in the course of history, but He will assess and judge them at the climax of history? And, in view of all that Yahweh sees and discerns (vv. 13-15), there will be no errors in judgment; judgment will be in complete accord with truth. And there is no 'secret stuff' that escapes notice.

I was browsing in a used bookstore some months back when I ran into a book by Iris Chang called *The Rape of Nanking*, an account of the atrocities the Japanese military perpetrated on the Chinese residents of Nanking, beginning in late 1937. Ms. Chang's motivation for writing this book lay in the almost conspiracy of silence about these horrors. Hitler's treatment of the Jews or the US' use of the atomic bomb received all kinds of press in connection with World War II, but somehow the crimes against Nanking lay buried in the historical landfill. She summarized some of the sufferings:

> Chinese men were used for bayonet practice and in decapitation contests. An estimated 20,000-80,000 Chinese women were raped. Many soldiers went beyond rape to disembowel women, slice off their breasts, nail them alive to walls. Fathers were forced to rape their daughters, and sons their mothers, as other family members watched. Not only did live burials, castration,

the carving of organs, and the roasting of people become routine, but more diabolical tortures were practiced, such as hanging people by their tongues on iron hooks or burying people to their waists and watching them get torn apart by German shepherds.[10]

But it was and has been all so relatively unnoticed. Yet the point of our psalm is that it *was* noticed. No 'curtain of silence' can obscure such deeds from the God of verses 13-15. Nor can it obscure the brutalities and cruelties committed against the 'people for his own possession' across our world every day of this twenty-first century. We may have perplexities over why justice lingers, but our psalm assures us that nothing is missed.

We ought then to praise our God for His work in the stuff we call history. He not only, we might say, sets up the game, He governs the playing field (v. 10). He both orders the flow of history (vv. 10-12) and will judge at the climax of history (vv. 13-15).

In verses 16-22 we meet a third reason for praise, **God's work in difficulty**. This section seems concerned with the troubles of God's people, of their need of deliverance from difficulties like death and famine (v. 19). But we're getting ahead of ourselves.

We must begin with verses 16-17. These are proverbial-type statements, but at first glance they don't seem to pack much wisdom. In fact, they may appear almost nonsensical. In any case, when he speaks of God's deliverance in our difficulties, the psalmist begins by *overturning conventional*

---

10   Iris Chang, *The Rape of Nanking* (New York: Basic Books, 1997), 6. See also pages 8, 87-88.

thinking (vv. 16-17). We tend to think that a huge army would be just the ticket for a king (v. 16a), massive strength the supreme advantage for a warrior (v. 16b), and that a horse (representing military materiel) would make one a sure winner, or at least a viable escapee (v. 17). In our translation, 'huge,' 'massive,' and 'great' all render *rab*, 'muchness.' So there's a big stress on abundant human power and resources; but even a stellar horse will prove *šeqer*, a lie ('utter disappointment'), for getting you out of a jam. But it simply doesn't make sense. This is not the way we tend to think.

But sometimes conventional thinking is wrong. When Theodore Roosevelt was a child, he was quite sickly and fragile. One major adversity was his asthma. Attacks would come and last for hours or days, wracking his frame and, if at night, stealing his sleep. There were various 'treatments' thought to alleviate the problem. In a letter young Teddy refers to one. He had been sitting up for four unsleeping hours, he said, and 'Papa made me smoke a cigar.'[11] Nicotine was thought by some to be effective against asthma. From our vantage point we nearly gag at the thought of a small lad gasping for breath and being told to take another drag on a cigar!

Conventional thinking, then, can be way off the mark. Armies and horses don't save. Just ask Pharaoh (Exod. 15:1, 4, 21). So what are God's people to do in their troubles? The psalmist says they must go on *confiding in unsleeping providence*, on God who always sees and works to deliver from death and destitution (vv. 18-19). When verse

---

11 H. W. Brands, *T.R.: The Last Romantic* (New York: Basic Books, 1997), 23.

18 speaks of the 'eye of Yahweh' it seems to be picking up the references from previous verses that speak of Yahweh 'looking down', 'seeing,' 'gazing down,' and 'discerning'. Only here the object of His gaze is 'those who fear him', who are 'waiting for his unfailing love' (v. 18).

There is a superb illustration of verses 18-19 in 2 Chronicles 16. That's part of the whole stretch of text (2 Chron. 14–16) about Asa, king of Judah. The whole story is twofold. In chapters 14–15 Judah is under attack from Zerah and a huge horde of Ethiopians and Libyans, but Asa was leaning on the everlasting arms (14:11) and God gave him a marvelous victory. But later, Baasha, king of Israel, to the north of Judah, began building fortifications at Ramah close to Judah's northern border. He was probably thinking of an economic blockade, cutting off access in and out of Judah (16:1). In face of this threat Asa turns to diplomacy. He takes funds from the temple and from his own royal treasury and sends an 'incentive' to the king of Syria, asking him to break the latter's treaty with Israel and to turn and attack Israel. The king of Syria is only too happy to be bought and overruns some of the northernmost cities of Israel. King Baasha has to leave off the brick-and-mortar work at Ramah and go off to deal with the military disaster to his rear. Relieved of this pressure, Asa and his people cart off Baasha's construction supplies at Ramah and use them to build two fortifications of their own. It was one slick move.

But Hanani the seer did not see it that way. He confronted King Asa and accused him of relying on the king of Syria rather than on Yahweh (16:7). He reminded Asa of how the king had previously relied on Yahweh in face of the massive Ethiopian onslaught and of how Yahweh had handed that army into Asa's power (16:8), and then he explained why: 'For Yahweh – his eyes keep roaming around through all the earth to show how strong he is with those whose hearts are loyal to him' (2 Chron. 16:9). Can you catch the 'tone' of that text? It's as if Yahweh patrols His world looking for opportunities to show His people how strong He is in their various troubles. That is the same teaching as in verse 18 of our psalm: 'Why, the eye of Yahweh is on those who fear him.' We do not escape or survive because we have amassed an array of human resources (Ps. 33:16-17), but because Yahweh's vigilant eye is keeping watch over us in these troubles (cf. Exod. 2:25; 3:7).

This text also raises questions for us, for there are any number of Yahweh's people in our world who seem to continue in their distress without seeing relief. And so we live with that mystery. But that does not negate the fact that so many of us owe Yahweh our praise for His work in our difficulties. My life has been rather ordinary so far, not really packed with breath-taking drama. And yet as I sit here this December afternoon writing on this text, memory multiplies instances in every segment of life when the watching eye of Yahweh was upon me to deliver and preserve. I begin to isolate two or three of them and suddenly a bunch more come cascading in. It would not be appropriate for me to specify and itemize them. But it clearly supports the way 2 Chronicles 16:9 speaks of it – Yahweh seems to have such an *enthusiasm* about this sort of thing. And that's why His people look to Him and 'wait' (verbs in vv. 18, 20, 22) for His unfailing love.

Psalm 34

Of David, when he changed his manner before Abimelech, so that he drove him away and he went off.

(1) I will bless Yahweh at all times;
his praise (will be) continually in my mouth.

(2) In Yahweh my soul makes its boast;
let the downtrodden hear and be glad.

(3) Magnify Yahweh with me,
and let us lift up his name together!

(4) I sought Yahweh, and he answered me,
and he delivered me from everything I dreaded.

(5) Those who look to him brighten up
– and may their faces not blush.

(6) This poor fellow cried, and **Yahweh** heard
– and saved him from all his troubles.

(7) The Angel of Yahweh keeps camping around those
who fear him – and rescues them.

(8) Taste and see how good Yahweh is!
Happy is the man who takes refuge in him.

(9) Fear Yahweh, you saints of his,
     for those who fear him lack nothing.

(10) Young lions are in need and famished,
     but those seeking Yahweh will never lack any good thing.

(11) Come, sons, listen to me;
     I will teach you fear of Yahweh.

(12) Who is the man who delights in life,
     who loves (many) days,
     (who wants) to see good?

(13) Keep your tongue from evil
     and your lips from speaking deceit.

(14) Turn away from evil and do good;
     seek peace – and pursue it.

(15) The eyes of Yahweh are toward the righteous
     and his ears – toward their cry for help.

(16) The face of Yahweh is against evildoers
         to cut off the memory of them from the earth.

(17) They cry – and **Yahweh** hears,
     and from all their distresses he delivers them.

(18) Yahweh is near to the broken-hearted,
     and saves those crushed in spirit.

(19) How many evils come to the righteous,
     but Yahweh will deliver him from all of them.

(20) He keeps all his bones,
     not one of them is broken.

(21) Evil will put the wicked to death,
     and those who hate the righteous will be condemned.

(22) Yahweh ransoms the life of his servants;
     none of those taking refuge in him will be condemned.

11

A Sane Meditation
on Deliverance

Imagine visiting the village of Ste.-Mere-Eglise in France a few years after World War II. You stand by the village church on the edge of the town square. You take it in from steps to steeple and may think little of it. But if Private John Steele of the US 82nd Airborne were with you, he would tell you there's a story behind that steeple. For in June 1944 he was among 13,000 men parachuting into France. Heavy winds, however, kept Steele and others from landing in the designated drop zones. He saw his parachute being swept toward this village where fires were burning and mayhem was afoot, as a panicked local German garrison was machine-gunning stray invaders. Then what seemed worse occurred and Steele's parachute caught on the church steeple – he was left dangling by the eaves. His knife slipped and sailed to earth as he tried to hack himself loose. He decided his best option was to feign death and to hang limply from his chute that was too close to the clanging church bell. He was 'dead' for over two hours until the chaos ceased, and he was cut down and taken captive by the Germans.[1] There is a story behind that steeple. It was, in a sense, Steele's salvation.

That is sometimes the way it is with a psalm. Occasionally the psalm has a 'heading', a scant one-liner that says, 'You know, there's a story behind this psalm.' Psalm 34 is like that. The heading points to the story behind it: 'Of David, when he changed his manner before Abimelech, so that he drove him away and he went off.' That account is in 1 Samuel 21:10-15. David is haunted, hated, and hunted by Saul. That David fled to Gath, a Philistine city where Achish ruled,[2] shows how terribly desperate he was. Perhaps he thought Achish would take him on as a mercenary. But David had been decimating Philistine troops, and then he shows up in Gath with Goliath's sword (cf. 1 Sam. 21:8-9)! It's the equivalent of a steer walking into a meat-processing plant. The Philistines apparently put David under arrest (cf. 'in their hands,' 1 Sam. 21:13). What to do? David acted like he'd lost his marbles. He scrawled on the doors of the town gates; he let his slobber and saliva slither down his beard. Maybe he gave blank or wild stares at his Philistine guards. Achish thought he already had his quota of 'whacko' specimens and so ordered David released. Now when we read 1 Samuel 21 we're tempted to exclaim, 'What a clever ruse!' But

---

1   See Cornelius Ryan, *The Longest Day* (New York: Simon and Schuster, 1959), 130-33.

2   'Abimelech' in the psalm heading is likely a dynastic name, whereas Achish is the king's personal name.

that's where Psalm 34 comes in. It was, says David, not human cleverness but divine deliverance. It was not a slick move but a matter of 'this poor fellow cried, and Yahweh heard' (v. 6). So we can look upon Psalm 34 as a sane meditation on Yahweh's deliverance.

The psalm is in the form of an alphabetical acrostic, each verse (almost always) beginning with the subsequent letter of the Hebrew alphabet. Though one cannot be certain, Ellison suggests that 'David was so moved by his escape that he felt the need of such artificial convention to discipline his feelings.'[3] At least it helped David think through his deliverance thoroughly, as it were from A to Z.

Since the psalm is an acrostic, it can be difficult to discern a pattern. It tends to look like a series of separate statements without much of a 'flow'. But I think there is an overall shape to it. I would divide it into two major parts: verses 1-10 are primarily testimony, while verses 11-22 are instruction. There are four 'from all' statements that keep the theme of the psalm before us:

'And he delivered me from everything [or: all] I
dreaded.' (v. 4)
'And saved him from all his troubles.' (v. 6)
'And from all their distresses he delivers them.' (v. 17)
'But Yahweh will deliver him from all of them.' (v. 19)

We begin, then, by looking at the **'Testimony'** (vv. 1-10). And the initial part of David's testimony consists of *boasting*: 'In Yahweh my soul makes its boast' (v. 2a). He

---

3   H. L. Ellison, *The Psalms*, Scripture Union Bible Study Books (Grand Rapids: Eerdmans, 1968), 31.

intends for this boasting and praise to be constant and ongoing ('at all times,' 'continually,' v. 1), encouraging ('let the downtrodden hear and be glad,' v. 2b), and, well, greedy (v. 3). This last is the plain implication of verse 3: 'Magnify Yahweh with me, and let us lift up his name together.' Praise is greedy, because it is always seeking to multiply itself; praise cannot be content to be solitary: it craves company. Praise is always covetous for more praise. It tries to be infectious. It's always after a *fellowship* of praise.

Such was the case that day in colonial America when John Witherspoon's neighbor burst into Witherspoon's office at the College of New Jersey. They both lived at Rock Hill, about two miles from the college. The breathless neighbor intrudes himself to exclaim, 'Dr. Witherspoon, you must join me in giving thanks to God for his extraordinary providence in saving my life!' The story tumbled out: he had been driving in; the horse spooked; the buggy was smashed to bits on the rocks, but he had escaped unharmed.[4] 'You must join me in giving thanks to God.' Praise has a conspiracy for more praise. Or I think of a recent request from one of our friends. She asked prayer for a missionary wanting to work in a European country. It seemed such an ideal fit. He had already served some years elsewhere, he was fluent in the language of the target group, so there would be no delay over acquiring a language. But he needed additional financial support

---

4   I think the story originally goes back to A. A. Hodge. Witherspoon made his own point in face of this report; see my *Joshua: No Falling Words* (Ross-shire: Christian Focus, 2000), 48-49.

to be permitted to go – and about two weeks in which to raise it. Would we pray? Several weeks later the word comes back: the Lord had heard and answered. Would we join in giving praise? That is typical of those who boast in Yahweh; they are always on the prowl for fellow-boasters.

His testimony also includes *remembering* (vv. 4-6). David conjures up and reports what Yahweh did for him in Gath:

> I sought Yahweh, and he answered me … (v. 4)
> This poor fellow cried, and Yahweh heard … (v. 6)

That deliverance is the fuel that feeds his praise. Praise is often like that: it rises out of remembering specific circumstances. And there is such a simplicity about it – notice the sequence of verbs: sought, answered, delivered (v. 4) and cried, heard, saved (v. 6).[5] That's the story in a nutshell. And verse 5 implies that not only David but many other believers find the same relief to be theirs: 'They look to him and they brighten up' (lit.).

Then, from 'remembering', David's testimony oozes over into *inferring* (vv. 7-10). That is, he draws some implications for all believers out of his account of his deliverance. As if he asks, 'Now are there some inferences we can read off my experience of Yahweh's rescue work?'

One is that His people enjoy Yahweh's protection (vv. 7-8). How does one explain deliverances like David's? Well, it must be that 'the Angel of Yahweh keeps camping

---

5   Verse 4b is a bit difficult. He speaks of all his 'dreads' or 'fears'. Is he delivered from what he dreads or from the dread he himself had about what he dreaded? Maybe both.

around those who fear him – and rescues them' (v. 7). Yahweh is One in whom a man can 'take refuge' (v. 8b). But what are we to make of this 'Angel of Yahweh'? We have met Him before in biblical narrative. His appearances in the book of Judges are instructive (Judg. 2:1-5; 6:11-24; 13:1-23). A careful reading of such passages indicates that the Angel of Yahweh is both distinct from Yahweh (appearing in human form) and yet identified with Yahweh. (Should we be *too* terribly surprised at the incarnation?). The Angel of Yahweh is how Yahweh appears when He wants specially to manifest Himself to His people. I sometimes say that the Angel of Yahweh is Yahweh Himself with His working clothes on.[6] And here He is near His people to rescue them. Indeed, He 'keeps camping around' them. The verb form is a participle, indicating ongoing action. This is not a fleeting or 'one-off' exercise for Him; this is what He does continuously. In all their sojournings God's people have Yahweh camping near them. Or maybe more than near – perhaps the text suggests 'camping around' wherever God's people are 'camping'. What Jacob called 'Mahanaim' – two camps (Gen. 32:1-2).

David also infers that Yahweh's servants enjoy His provision (vv. 9-10): 'those who fear him lack nothing' (v. 9b). 'Young lions,' lions in their prime, may not fare so well (v. 10a), 'but those seeking Yahweh will never lack any good thing' (v. 10b). Whatever is good for us God will see that we have. It's somewhat close to Matthew 7:9-11: we can be assured our Father will not play cruel games

---

6 See the discussion by Geerhardus Vos, *Biblical Theology* (Grand Rapids: Eerdmans, 1954), 85-89.

with us but give us 'good things'. Or we can simply stay in the Old Testament:

> For Yahweh God is sun and shield;
> Yahweh will give grace and glory;
> he will not hold back anything good
>> from those walking whole-heartedly (Ps. 84:11).

Now stand back and look over this 'testimony' again. We've tracked it in a sequence of boasting, remembering, and inferring. There's a buzz word some folks like to use in their writing: trajectory. (It sounds so much more sophisticated than 'path'). So do you see the trajectory here? What begins in praise (vv. 1-3, 4-6) ends up in assurance (vv. 7-10). So often the two go hand in hand. When I was a small lad I used to like to go with my father when he had to take our auto in for repairs. He went to a mechanic he knew in one of the former congregations he had served as pastor. It was only fourteen miles to Clarence Greenlee's garage. But after Clarence had repaired our car and before we left the town, my father would always stop near the bridge that had a steel floor in it (and made your tires 'whine') where the Vengold Ice Cream Factory was. We'd each get an ice cream cone. They always went together: Greenlee's garage and ice cream. And that's the pattern here: praise and assurance go together.

Haven't you found this to be so? Let's say you join the congregation in singing 'I Greet Thee, Who My Sure Redeemer Art.' You get to the fourth stanza:

> Thou hast the true and perfect gentleness,
> no harshness hast thou and no bitterness,

and what might happen? Might not a wave of assurance sweep over you, as you grasp afresh, 'Yes, that is precisely what my Savior is like, clearly shown in the way He has always dealt with me.' It is praise, but out of the praise flows this renewed sense of the steady kindness of your Redeemer. Or you are using Joachim Neander's 'Praise to the Lord, the Almighty.' It's clearly a hymn consumed with praise and yet how assurance oozes out of it when you sing, 'How oft in grief, hath not he brought thee relief....' We praise because Yahweh ought to be praised and thanked and blessed, but that praise tends to spill over into the often empty buckets of our need, assuring us that we have a protecting and providing God. Of course, a reverse implication is also possible: if our assurance is lacking it may be that our praise has been deficient.

The second segment of the psalm begins in verse 11, as David turns to give overt instruction. There were already hints of instruction in the 'testimony' section (e.g., vv. 8-9), but now he explicitly turns 'teacher'. In verses 11-22 we have this **instruction**.

David divides his instruction into two 'chunks,' the way of the righteous (vv. 11-14) and the way of Yahweh (vv. 15-22). He begins with an invitation:

Come, sons, listen to me;
I will teach you fear of Yahweh (v. 11).

'Fear of Yahweh' here is almost a stock phrase for 'faithful biblical religion'. Following this invitation David poses a question – Who would love a long life and like to enjoy good in it (v. 12)? Then he lays down his 'formula' for many and good days:

> Keep your tongue from evil
> and your lips from speaking deceit.
> Turn away from evil and do good;
> seek peace – and pursue it (vv. 13-14).

That is the way of the righteous; that is how the faithful should live. It consists of (1) control of your speech (v. 13); (2) the transformed direction of your life (v. 14a); and (3) your passion for peace (v. 14b). Perhaps that's not absolutely everything that 'fear of Yahweh' (v. 11b) covers, but it's a workable starter kit.

It's fascinating that Peter takes over verses 12-16a in his first epistle. One large hunk of his epistle (1 Pet. 2:11–4:19) deals with Christians' behavior. He strikes the keynote in 2:11-12, urging that believers keep their behavior 'attractive' among the pagans around them, and the Christian must do this, he says, (1) in his relationships (2:13–3:12), (2) in his conflicts (3:13–4:6), (3) in his times (4:7-11; cf. 7a), and (4) in his expectations (4:12-19). Peter brings Psalm 34 into play in the first category of the Christian's relationships (2:13–3:12). The key expression in that section is 'be submissive', whether to human government, masters, or husbands (2:13, 18; 3:1), after which he sums up (3:8) his argument and clinches it by quoting Psalm 34:12-16a in 1 Peter 3:10-12. It's as if he says, at least in part, 'Here in Psalm 34 is a clip that shows you what "an attractive way of life" (1 Pet. 2:12) is.'

This is 'the way of the righteous', as applicable to the New Testament Christian as to the Old Testament believer.

But now (back to the psalm) David describes 'the way of Yahweh' (vv. 15-22). There is a connection between verses 11-14 and verses 15-22. We might ask, 'But why should we live that way? Why the carefulness, truthfulness, and integrity of speech? Why maintain a consistent, godly direction in our living? Why seek to live without rancor in relation to others? What incentives are there for such living?' I think verses 15-22 supply these. That is, it's as if there is a causal connection between verses 15-22 and verses 11-14. Here in the psalm it is implicit. There is no 'Now the reason you live this way is because...' at the beginning of verse 15. But note 1 Peter 3 again. Note that Peter has a 'because' before 'the eyes of the Lord are upon the righteous' (v. 15a in the psalm). So Peter makes explicit what is implicit in the psalm. What Yahweh does in verses 15-22 supplies the incentive to live as verses 13-14 direct.

Can we unpack the way of Yahweh? Of what does it consist? For a start it has to do with the anatomy of your God (vv. 15-17). David refers to the eyes (cf. 33:18), ears, and face of Yahweh (vv. 15-16) and that He 'hears' the cry of His people (v. 17). It's his way of expressing the attention Yahweh has for His people (v. 15) and the opposition He shows to the wicked (v. 16). Noting Yahweh's eyes, ears, and face suggests that Yahweh bends His whole being to His people's welfare.

Along the same lines, verses 18-20 speak of the closeness of His care. 'Yahweh is near to the brokenhearted, and saves the crushed in spirit' (v. 18).

How are we to understand these conditions? As specifically brokenhearted and crushed over sin (Ps. 51:17), or more generally, as brokenhearted and crushed by opposition (Ps. 69:20) or perhaps by circumstances observed (Jer. 23:9) or perhaps endured? I think the sense is of being brokenhearted and crushed by circumstances they have had to endure. 'From all their distresses he delivers them' in verse 17 seems to support this option. There is no cover-up of the need – they are brokenhearted and crushed. Indeed, verse 19a is nothing but realism – 'How many evils come to the righteous.' There is no ducking the truth of the trouble. And yet strong assurance meets this sober realism (vv. 19b-20). If we include verse 17, we come under a barrage of 'alls':

> And from *all* their distresses he delivers them (17b)
> But Yahweh will deliver him from *all* of them (19b)
> He keeps *all* his bones... (20)

We might pause to ask how this can be so. The text does not fuzzy over the troubles (vv. 18-19a), but do these assurances promise too much? Clearly, the main point is that Yahweh preserves His people in face of and in spite of all their afflictions. Perhaps the 'solution' is found in Jesus' paradox in Luke 21:16, 18. He tells His disciples that they will be betrayed by those closest them and that 'they will put some of you to death' (v. 16b) – then turns round and says, 'Yet not a hair of your head will perish' (v. 18). In any case, here in the psalm, 'Yahweh is near' (v. 18a) and that is what matters. If the disciples had thought a little, perhaps they would have realized that if Jesus was in the boat with them (Mark 4:38), they were likely safe enough.

The last segment of the 'way of Yahweh' has to do with the assurance of your destiny (vv. 21-22). Here we are dealing with ultimate things, with the final standing of the wicked and Yahweh's servants respectively. The verb here has the idea of being held guilty or being condemned. 'Those who hate the righteous will be condemned' (v. 21b). But the opposite of condemnation is justification, and this is what Yahweh's servants are promised: 'None of those taking refuge in him will be condemned' (v. 22b). What assurance could be more highly prized? There's a story in John Whitecross's collection about a man named Reynolds from Bristol. A friend of his begged him to sit for his portrait. At length he consented. Then the questions: 'How would you like to be painted?' 'Sitting among books.' 'Any book in particular?' 'The Bible.' 'Open at what part?' 'At the fifth chapter of the Romans; the first verse to be legible: "Therefore, being justified by faith, we have peace with God through our Lord Jesus Christ."'[7] Oh, yes, the first verse to be legible – by all means! That's just an 'update' of Psalm 34:22. And there is no anchor like that.

Here in Psalm 34, then, we have testimony and instruction. Its setting (cf. the heading) is dramatic, but the psalm as such is rather sedate and calm. Yet how life-changing it proved to be for one John Cennick. Cennick was born in 1718, the youngest of seven children, into

---

7   *The Shorter Catechism Illustrated* (1828; reprint ed., London: Banner of Truth, 1968), 57.

a staunch Church of England home. He had rebelled and run wild in his early teens but in his later teen years came under intense agony of soul. For over two years he endured Spirit-induced misery and fear and anguish over his lost condition. Then, in his nineteenth year, the sun broke through. Skevington Wood tells of it:

> It was at an ordinary church service that the great illumination occurred and through the application of the healing Word. On Sunday, 6th September, 1737, the Psalm for the day was the thirty-fourth: 'Great are the troubles of the righteous, but the Lord delivereth him out of them all; and they that put their trust in Him shall not be destitute.' No sooner had the singing ended than the burden was removed from his soul and he found a glad deliverance.[8]

An ordinary church service. The 34th Psalm. Glad deliverance. Thanks be to God!

---

8 A. Skevington Wood, *The Inextinguishable Blaze* (Grand Rapids: Eerdmans, 1968), 155-56.

Psalm 35

Of David.

(1)   Contend, Yahweh, with those contending with me,
      fight with those fighting against me.

(2)   Take hold of small shield and body shield
        and rise up as my help,

(3)   and draw out (the) spear
      and close in to meet my pursuers.
      Say to my soul,
         'I am your salvation!'

(4)   Let them be ashamed and humiliated
        who seek after my life;
      let them be turned back and abashed
        who scheme disaster for me.

(5)   Let them be like chaff before the wind
      with the Angel of Yahweh driving (them) along.

(6)   Let their way be all dark and slippery
      with the Angel of Yahweh pursuing them.

(7)   Because for no reason they have hidden
        their netted-pit for me,
      for no reason they have dug (it) to take my life.

(8) Let ruin he is not aware of come on him,
and let his net which he hid capture him
   – let him fall into it in ruin.

(9) And my soul will exult in Yahweh;
it will rejoice in his salvation.

(10) All my bones will say, 'Yahweh, who is like you
   – delivering the afflicted one from the one too strong for him,
even the afflicted and needy from the one who is robbing him?'

(11) Vicious witnesses rise up;
what I know nothing of they demand of me.

(12) They pay me back evil for good
   – I am utterly alone!

(13) But I, when they were sick
   – sackcloth was my clothing;
I afflicted myself with fasting;
and my prayer would come back to me.

(14) I went round as for a friend, as for my brother,
like mourning for a mother I bowed down in mourning.

(15) But when I stumbled they were glad,
and they gathered round
   – they gathered against me,
     assailants I didn't know
   – they tore at me and didn't stop;

(16) as godless mockers at table
   – gnashing their teeth at me.

(17) Lord, how long will you look on?
Bring me back from the ruin they intend,
   my very life from the lions.

(18) I will give you thanks in the vast assembly,
among a numerous people I will praise you.

(19) Do not let those who are wrongfully my enemies
      rejoice over me;
   (do not let) those who hate me for no reason
      wink the eye.

(20) For it's not peace that they speak,
   but against those who are quiet in the land
      they scheme with words of deceit.

(21) So they opened wide their mouths against me;
   they said, 'Aha! Aha! Our eyes have seen (it)!'

(22) You have seen, Yahweh, do not be silent;
   O Lord, do not be far from me.

(23) Stir (yourself) up and awake for the right decision about me,
   (awake), my God and my Lord, for my case.

(24) Decide about me in line with your righteousness,
      Yahweh, my God,
   and do not let them rejoice over me.

(25) Don't let them say in their heart,
    'Aha! Just what we wanted!'
   Don't let them say,
    'We have swallowed him up!'

(26) Let those be ashamed and abashed together
      who rejoice over my disaster;
   let them be covered with shame and humiliation
      who magnify (themselves) against me.

(27) Let them shout for joy and be glad
      who delight in my vindication,
   and let them say continually,
    'How great Yahweh is,
    who delights in the welfare of his servant.'

(28) And my tongue will utter your righteousness
    – your praise all day long.

The Fighter

12

I had a problem in my family. At the time we had two sons, the older was maybe five or six, the younger three or four. The older was mostly even-keeled and content, the younger more aggressive with more 'fire' inside. So the younger would sometimes attack or hit the older, but the older son wouldn't retaliate. That made for a problem. Of course, I could discipline the younger son for – as they say in American football – 'unnecessary roughness.' But there was a far easier solution. Several times I told the older son how to deal with attacks from his brother. 'Just slug him,' I would beg. He was the bigger of the two, and, if he would just hit back once, the younger one would learn his lesson and cease and desist. You may be appalled at my parenting,[1] but 'this is my story, and I'm sticking to it.'

---

1   I haven't space here to expound Matthew 5:38-42, but suffice to say it does not teach that we are to be wimps for Jesus.

I was trying to teach our son that he needed to be a *fighter*. And sometimes that is what we need Yahweh to be. And that's where Psalm 35 comes in.

Let's get a map of Psalm 35 in front of us before we wade through the teaching. The psalm breaks into three sections, verses 1-10, 11-18, and 19-28, with each section closing with a vow to praise (vv. 9-10, 18, and 28 respectively). Certain distinct emphases stand out. In verses 1-10 David stresses his danger, in 11-18 the heartlessness and ingratitude of his enemies (note vv. 12-16), and in 19-28 the tragedy of their possible success (note vv. 24-25). We'll follow these divisions in the exposition and couch the main headings in words that David might have used.

We can call verses 1-10 **the scenario I suggest**. This section depicts, we could say, the ideal that David would like to see come about: how he'd like Yahweh to show Himself (vv. 1-3), what he'd like to happen to his enemies (vv. 4-8), and the response of praise he would then be glad to offer (vv. 9-10).

Do you see what a bracing view of God he has?

Contend, Yahweh, with those contending with me,
fight with those fighting against me.
Take hold of small shield and body shield
    and rise up as my help,
and draw out (the) spear
and close in to meet my pursuers.
Say to my soul,
    'I am your salvation!' (vv. 1-3).

Do you see how he thinks about Yahweh? Here is no namby-pamby deity. He wants a fighter, One who comes, takes up the cudgels for His servant, enters into the fray, and hollers, 'I will get you victory!' Yahweh is a warrior. This rather shocks us perhaps, given the soft and sentimental attitudes awash even sometimes in our church culture. But, my, how refreshing it is when someone sports such a lively view of God.

Sometimes we need a bit of a shock to get us to think properly. We can, for example, almost glamorize the death of Christians, perhaps especially martyrs. That's when it's helpful to hear Luther:

> I don't like to see examples of joyful death. On the other hand, I like to see those who tremble and shake and grow pale when they face death and yet get through. It was so with the great saints; they were not glad to die.[2]

Such a view may not be what we're used to hearing or expect to hear and so it may bother us at first – but it forces us to think, and then we begin to think that what first strikes us as odd may be true. Or what about the way John 'Rabbi' Duncan prayed in nineteenth-century Scotland? The Privy Council was in the habit of holding its meetings on the Lord's Day. So in one of his closing prayers, Duncan's petition was:

> O Lord, bless our sinful, godless, Sabbath-breaking Privy Council. Thou knowest that Thou art not honoured

---

2 *Luther's Works*, vol. 54: Table Talk (Philadelphia: Fortress, 1967), 65.

there, for they profane Thy holy day by their meetings for State business.[3]

Surely, someone might say, he didn't pray like that! No, but he did. And once you get past the initial surprise you realize it was perfectly proper. So here with David's view of Yahweh. 'Draw out the spear.' 'Close in to meet my pursuers.' 'Fight with those fighting against me.' Yahweh is no celestial marshmallow, no mere psychological pacifier, but a warrior who plunges into combat for His servants.

Next, David lays out how he envisions God's work, that is, the results he wants to see when Yahweh fights for him (vv. 4-8). This is the 'scenario' he wants to see. He wants those seeking to wipe him out to 'be ashamed and humiliated' (v. 4). He pictures his desire for them: he wants them to be blown away like the wind whips away the useless chaff from the threshing-floor (v. 5); he wants them sliding down into a dark and disastrous ruin (v. 6). The reason for this is that they have conspired against him 'for no reason' (v. 7). That phrase translates *ḥinnām* (used twice in verse 7; once also in verse 19b). It means 'without cause'; David means there is simply no justification for their enmity.[4] So he is perplexed. Why are they seeking to annihilate him? Hence David asks Yahweh to bring

---

3 A. Moody Stuart, *The Life of John Duncan* (1872; reprint ed., Edinburgh: Banner of Truth, 1991), 31.

4 Yahweh uses this term when speaking to Satan in Job 2:3, after Satan had devastated all that Job had: '... and still he keeps holding fast to his whole-heartedness, though you've incited me against him, to swallow him up for no reason.' Yahweh suggests that His servants may endure suffering for which there is no adequate reason (except perhaps to vindicate Yahweh).

about the supreme irony: they have spread a camouflage net over a pit to catch and destroy him (v. 7), so let his enemy fall to ruin in his very own net and pit (v. 8). God's judgments can have such ironic twists. It's something like what happened when Mark Twain's *Huckleberry Finn* was published. The Concord, Massachusetts' public library dubbed it as 'trash, suitable only for slums.' That obviously incited public curiosity and increased sales. Twain noted that because they had cast Huck out as 'trash', it would sell 25,000 copies for sure.[5]

Should Yahweh bring about the scenario David sketches in verses 4-8, he then indicates how he plans to respond in the first of the 'vows of praise' (vv. 9-10). 'My soul will exult in Yahweh,' he says in verse 9, and then in verse 10: 'All my bones will say....' He does not mean that only his hard, structural skeleton will praise; 'all my bones' is a way of saying 'my whole being'. And he will praise for what is a nearly 'impossible' salvation: 'Yahweh, who is like you – delivering the afflicted one from the one too strong for him, even the afflicted and needy from the one who is robbing him' (v. 10). Such a deliverance surely calls for total-bones-praise!

Does Yahweh still fight for His people? Yes, but it may not always be with shield and spear as David envisioned. Let me pass on an instance that came to me through Sudan Interior Mission materials. In an African country Hassan was complaining against his wife, Sonya, who planned to go to a Christian women's conference. Who will cook,

---

5   Seymour Morris, Jr., *American History Revised* (New York: Broadway Books, 2010), 123.

who will clean?, he griped. Then the blows came down on her. Before dawn on the Monday morning Sonya quietly left for the church conference. By mid-morning Hassan was up. He stood on the front porch and yelled, 'Good riddance! See this? It is that woman's only key to my house. And she will never come in again.' His neighbors saw Hassan fling the key into the river that flowed by their homes. He then stormed down the road to spend the week with his mistress. At the conference others prayed with and for Sonya and her frightful marital situation. On Friday, Sonya returned, stopped at the market on the way home – she wanted to have a fine meal for Hassan when he returned from prayers at the mosque. She found the house locked up tight. So she began cleaning the fish outside. As she cut it open, she discovered something hard in its belly. It was a key. She hollered to her neighbor, 'This looks really familiar!' Her neighbor's eyes grew wide. Sonya tried the lock. The key slid right in! True to form, Hassan was livid when he came home and found Sonya inside. He demanded to know how she had gotten in. She explained about the house key inside the fish. Hassan became quiet. Sunday morning, he asked to join her at church. After the service he told the pastor, 'I want to serve the God of the Christians. He is the One who knows and has power to do what no one else can.' It was an 'impossible' piece of work – 'delivering the afflicted one from the one too strong for him.' Yahweh fights for David but also for an abused and beleaguered African wife; sometimes He may fight with shield and spear (vv. 2-3), but he can also fight with fish and keys. The last stanza of a hymn ('Fear Not, O Little Flock') sums it up well:

Amen, Lord Jesus, grant our pray'r;
great Captain, now your arm make bare,
fight for us once again;
so shall your saints and martyrs raise
a mighty chorus to your praise,
world without end. Amen.[6]

In the second section David gives us a clearer picture of his trouble as he relates **the betrayal I experience** (vv. 11-18). He calls his opponents, literally, 'witnesses of violence' (v. 11a). He says, 'What I know nothing of they demand of me' (v. 11b). That's a bit puzzling but may well mean that they try to get him to confess to crimes he has not committed and knows nothing about.[7] The heart of the trouble is that 'they pay me back evil for good' (v. 12a), and he goes on to give an extended description of that (vv. 13-16).

David tells then of his intense concern for these current opponents when, at some time in the past, they were apparent friends and associates. They were sick (v. 13a) and he was deeply affected. He went so far as to wear grieving duds (sackcloth) and committed himself to fasting and prayer in their behalf. There are about four different views of what the last line of verse 13 means ('and my prayer would come back to me'), but I think the best option contextually is to assume it means something like: my prayer would keep coming back to my memory,

---

6   Trinity Hymnal (1990), No. 566.
7   J. A. Alexander, *The Psalms Translated and Explained* (1864; reprint ed., Grand Rapids: Zondervan, n.d.), 151. Cf. NLT: 'They accuse me of crimes I know nothing about.'

reminding me that I needed to pray for them again and again. Everyone could see he was weighted down with grief as for a close friend or relative (v. 14). But all this carried no weight when David himself 'stumbled' (v. 15a), whether through illness or some other mishap or trouble. All their malice and pent-up hatred found vent as they licked their chops over his imminent demise. Even men David didn't know (v. 15c) joined their ranks. Opposition from enemies is one thing, but betrayal by those who once stood beside you slices out a bit of your guts.

Even *reading* about betrayal disturbs one. Recently I was working through a biography of Henry Clay. He ran for the US presidency several times. In 1840 he was the clear front-runner for the Whig party nomination. William Seward, New York's governor, told Clay that the latter's election would be most gratifying to him. John Tyler of Virginia expressed 'great solicitude' for Clay's obtaining the presidency. Thurlow Weed, Whig party boss in New York, drowned Clay in smiles whenever they met, told him of his 'warm' support, and called Clay his 'personal preference' over all other Whig candidates. But it was all duplicity. Seward, Tyler, and Weed all considered Clay a political liability, and even as they proclaimed their support, they were conspiring to keep Clay from gaining the party nomination.[8] And they succeeded. Now Henry Clay was no squeaky-clean paragon of virtue, but there is still something about the deviousness and deception of his professed supporters that turns one's stomach.

---

8   H. G. Unger, *Henry Clay* (Boston: Da Capo, 2015), 207-09.

The betrayal, however, is not the psalmist's only, or even the most grievous, problem. He also has to face divine delay: 'Lord, how long will you look on?' (v. 17a). Yahweh seems to be standing on the sidelines, more like a spectator than a deliverer. David pleads for that deliverance-work (v. 17b), and by his promise of praise (v. 18) he expects that deliverance to come. But at the present moment, nothing has changed, Yahweh is still 'looking on', and the mockers (v. 16) seem to have carried the day. Human betrayal and divine delay are a lethal combination.

Christian believers, however, because of our location in redemptive history, may have stronger hope here. For we are aware that the God of Psalm 35 has come to us and Himself suffered betrayal. It's like reading from a billboard every time we partake of the Lord's supper: 'The Lord Jesus, on the night in which he was betrayed, took bread...' (1 Cor. 11:23). It doesn't mean we won't ever be troubled by God's delays – even on this side of the empty tomb we often face that mystery. But it does seem to make a difference to know that the Lord who 'looks on' (v. 17) has nevertheless been through betrayal Himself, 'who has in every way been tempted, exactly as we have been' (Heb. 4:15, TCNT). Because we have such a Lord, we can be confident of giving Him thanks 'in the vast assembly' (v. 18).

Finally, David speaks of **the vindication I crave** (vv. 19-28). There is a latent fear that pervades this closing section. Three times David prays his enemies will not 'rejoice over me' (vv. 19, 24) or 'over my disaster' (v. 26). Or he can express the same thing differently: don't let them 'wink the eye' (v. 19b), a signal by which they congratulate one another on their success; or very clearly in verse 25: Don't let them say 'Just what we wanted!' or 'We have swallowed him up!' This segment is laced with a fear of the enemies' throwing parties and celebrating the downfall of God's servant.

No question then about his desperate need, but the way David expresses that need may be a bit surprising. Note again verses 23-24:

Stir (yourself) up and awake for the right decision about me,
(awake), my God and my Lord, for my case.

Decide about me in line with your righteousness,
          Yahweh, my God....

Legal language here. He wants God to pay attention to his 'case'. He wants Him to awake to give 'the right decision about me' (lit., 'for my judgment'); he wants Him to 'decide about me' (lit., 'judge me'), 'in line with your righteousness.' Here (v. 24) he speaks of Yahweh's righteousness; in verse 27 the saints speak of (lit.) 'my [David's] righteousness,' that is, David's vindication (my translation) – that is, his being shown by God to be in the right. He is not merely wanting deliverance or escape. Oh, he wants that, but he wants *more*. By delivering him he wants Yahweh to show that He was for him, that God thought David was in the right. Perhaps even more than rescue, David wanted vindication.

God's suffering servants often do not enjoy such vindication in this age. One grieves to look round our world and hear of believers in Nigeria simply gunned down in droves by either Fulani herdsmen or Boko Haram thugs; or of primarily Christian tribes attacked (even from the air) by the Burmese (= Myanmar) military; or of Al-Shabab terrorists stopping buses in Kenya, identifying the Christian passengers, and gunning them down. The litany is nearly endless. And their vindication waits – for another day (Rev. 6:9-11).

However, if David is vindicated in his crisis, not only will he himself praise Yahweh 'all day long' (v. 28), but God's people would receive tremendous encouragement and would say, 'How great Yahweh is, who delights in the welfare of his servant' (v. 27b). When God shows He is for David, not only is David rescued but saints are heartened. There is a 'spillover'.

This reminds me of Andree de Jongh, a young Belgian girl, who during World War II arranged escapes and escorted to safety British airmen who had been shot down over northwestern Europe. Part of her turf was Nazi-occupied France. Few of the fugitives she would accompany knew the French language and so whenever police or other officials might approach, her airman would suddenly find himself locked in a 'sultry embrace' with Andree![9] Passing themselves off as just another couple of ardent French lovers – until the danger passed. Look at it from the airman's perspective – it's a 'spillover' situation. Not only is a young lady leading him to safety but under certain conditions he gets to passionately kiss her! More is involved than he initially imagined. That is the way it is

---

9   W. E. Armstrong, 'The Lifeline Called Comet,' in *True Stories of Great Escapes* (Pleasantville, NY: Readers Digest, 1977), 79-83.

in Psalm 35. If David is delivered and defended, all God's people will be fortified and revel in praising Yahweh.

On the whole, contemporary believers distance themselves from the vigorous and virile expressions of faith, as found in Psalm 35. But what good is an effeminate faith (those last two words are almost a contradiction in terms)? There is that story of a delegation that went to see President Lincoln during the US War between the States. These men were pleading with him to dismiss General Grant because of his rumored drinking problem. Lincoln, however, had been eternally frustrated with his Union generals – somehow they never got around to fighting battles. So Lincoln stiff-armed his visitors' requests with: 'I can't spare this man – he fights!' In the same way Yahweh's people should look at the opening verses of Psalm 35 and take heart. Many of them in our time and world are hammered and hated, condemned and crushed, but they can look at the psalm and say, 'I can't do without this God – He fights!'

Psalm 36

For the music director. Of the servant of Yahweh, David.

(1) Rebellion speaks to the wicked in the depth of his heart;
     there is no dread of God before his eyes.

(2) For it soothes him in his eyes
         about finding out his guilt – to hate it.

(3) The words of his mouth – wickedness and deceit;
     he has ceased acting wisely, doing good.

(4) He plans **wickedness** on his bed;
     he takes his stand by a way that's not good;
     he does not reject evil.

(5) Yahweh – your unchanging love is in the heavens;
     your faithfulness (reaches) all the way up to the clouds!

(6) Your righteousness is like the highest mountains,
     your decisions are a vast deep;
     man and beast you save, Yahweh!

(7) How precious is your unchanging love, O God!
     And the sons of man can take refuge
         in the shadow of your wings.

(8) They take their fill from the richness of your house;
     and you give them drink from the wadi of your delights.

(9) For with you (is) the fountain of life;
     in your light we see light.

(10) Make your unchanging love go on (and on)
          for those who know you;
     and [make] your righteousness [go on and on]
          for the upright of heart.

(11) Don't let the foot of arrogance get to me;
     don't let the hand of the wicked drive me away.

(12) There the workers of wickedness have fallen!
     They have been slammed down and are unable to rise.

Unchanging Love
Changes Everything

13

For many years John Murray served as Professor of Systematic Theology at Westminster Seminary in Philadelphia. He often spent Sundays in the home of his pastor, and Calvin Freeman, a son of the manse, remembers how Murray would teach him and his brother Bible lessons on Sunday afternoons. He remembered lessons from Genesis about Abraham and Mr. Murray talking about 'Mesopotamia' in connection with Abraham. Murray apparently had a love affair with that word. He would say, 'I don't believe there is another word that has the same sound and beauty.'[1] Perhaps we'd have to agree; the word does 'flow' rather richly and elegantly.

Were it possible I believe David would have quoted John Murray – in part. In Psalm 36 he seems to say,

---

1   Iain H. Murray, 'Life of John Murray,' in *Collected Writings of John Murray: Volume 3* (Edinburgh: Banner of Truth, 1982), 73.

'I don't believe there is another word that has the same sound and beauty,' but he is referring to *ḥesed*. That is the delightful Hebrew word that can give translators fits. It's difficult to translate with only one word – some are used to ESV/RSV's 'steadfast love'. It's love, but love with an 'umph'. I've sometimes called it love with super-glue on it. It's Yahweh's love that simply won't let go. I've translated it variously even in this series of expositions; here in Psalm 36 I've used 'unchanging love'. That's *ḥesed*; that's the word David is so enamored with here in our psalm (vv. 5, 7, and 10).

While there are more elaborate breakdowns of the psalm, I think it best to take it in three main divisions. It moves from description (vv. 1-4) to confession (i.e., confession not of sin but of truth, vv. 5-9) to petition (vv. 10-12). Let's wend our way through the text using these rather colorlessly pedantic heads.

First, then, note his **description** (vv. 1-4). But what David describes is enough to curdle your insides and the Hebrew he uses is enough to baffle interpretation. He takes the first four verses simply to describe the wicked man. Maybe not the best way to 'sell' a psalm.

Here then is the wicked, and he first speaks of *the authority he receives* (v. 1a). The text is difficult. Literally, it is: 'Oracle of rebellion to the wicked in the depth of his heart.'[2] Of course oftentimes oracles are said to be from Yahweh but here it is 'rebellion' that delivers its 'revelation' to the wicked. It takes hold; it is 'in the depth

---

2   Suffice to say, my translation ('his heart,' not 'my heart') follows the reading of a few other Hebrew manuscripts.

of his heart'. Rather than being governed by any word of Yahweh, he listens to the voice of 'rebellion'. That, is his authority.

Then David speaks of *the restraint he rejects* (v. 1b). 'There is,' he says, 'no dread of God before his eyes.' The word for 'dread' is *paḥad* (dread, terror) which is something like fear on steroids.[3] Nothing holds this wicked fellow back. He has no dread of facing God's judgment. Nothing deters him from giving himself over to whatever evil he cooks up. Sometimes, like Abraham, we think of fear as a restraint. In Genesis 20 Abimelech dresses down Abraham for lying to him about Sarah, passing her off as only his sister. He asks Abraham why on earth he did such a thing. Abraham tells him that he thought 'there is clearly no fear of God in this place' (Gen. 20:11) and that they would kill him to get his wife. The word for 'fear' here is the more common one but the conceptual freight is still there. Abraham assumes that some fear of God acts as a deterrent to violence, but if that is absent, then anything goes. And he thought it was absent. Here in the psalm David implies that since the wicked has no dread of God there is no restraint to his viciousness.

Now there appears to be a companion-piece to this 'no dread of God' element. The Hebrew is a bit rough in verse 2, but it highlights *the immunity he imagines*. I have translated rather literally: 'For it soothes him in his eyes about finding out his guilt – to hate it.' He doesn't believe he will ever face consequences for the ruin he causes. Notice the 'it' – 'it soothes him in his eyes.' Motyer points

---

3   See Andrew Bowling's article in *TWOT*, 2:720-21.

out that the 'it' is the 'word' or 'oracle' that directs him in verse 1a.[4] But it's all so subjective. 'It soothes him *in his eyes*,' that is, in his own estimation, in his own thinking. It has no more 'authority' than his own 'wannabe'. But he assumes he is free from all comeuppance and that sets him 'free' to inflict all sorts of harm.

In verses 3-4 David goes on to speak of *the abandonment he practices*. He simply 'gives himself up' – if it were King Ahab we could say he 'sells himself to do evil' (1 Kings 21:20). The statements of the text are clear:

> 'He has ceased acting wisely, doing good.' (v. 3b)
> 'He plans wickedness on his bed...' (v. 4a)
> 'He does not reject evil.' (v. 4c)

This 'abandonment' dominates both his speech (v. 3a) and his action (v. 3b). It consumes his thinking (v. 4a) – even in bed he does not rest but conspires to carry out his next devastating attack.

Now why does David begin his psalm this way? It's terribly depressing to wade through four verses like this right from the start. Is he not trying to say to fellow believers, 'Take a good, hard look. This is your world. These are the sorts of characters you will be facing.'? The church of Christ today is either facing or under people like this. Even if there are not direct attacks on the church (and there are cascades of those), God's people still meet the deceitfulness (v. 3a) and the scheming (v. 4a) of governments. In the wake of the 2016 Religion Law in

---

4   Alec Motyer, *Psalms by the Day* (Ross-shire: Christian Focus, 2016), 91-92.

Russia, believers are facing official government threats to close and demolish their churches or prayer houses unless they can obtain 'registration' to make them legal. But the 'registration' game (a problem in a number of 'republics') might simply be the creative scheme that godless bureaucrats dream up on their beds (cf. v. 4a). If believers try to register, they may be told they need at least 300 or 500 on the rolls for a kosher registration, or they need to file more papers, or submit names and addresses of members – a never-ending hopeless process. Not the most vicious opposition perhaps but part of the opposition of the wicked who love to *toy* with the saints and increase their misery.

Back in the late 1940s in American baseball Jackie Robinson became the first black player in the major leagues. He played for the (then) Brooklyn Dodgers, and breaking the 'color line' in pro baseball was clearly no picnic for him. Pee Wee Reese, the Dodgers' shortstop, was a faithful advocate and firm supporter of Robinson in those critical days. Once Robinson was raging about how many knock-down pitches he had to face. Opposing pitchers seemed to delight to throw at him when he was batting. But Pee Wee Reese tempered Robinson's anger a bit by saying: 'Jack, some guys are th'owing at you because you're black and that's a terrible thing. But there are other guys, Jack, who are th'owing at you because they plain don't like you.'[5] That is what's behind verses 1-4. It's not a theoretical sketch but a realistic portrayal of the sort of

---

5   Roger Kahn, *Into My Own* (New York: Thomas Dunne, 2006), 107.

villainy God's people continually face. David is trying to tell you that there are some who plain don't like you.

The second section, verses 5-9, we call **confession**, meaning a confession of truth in this case, not of sin. And what a contrast to verses 1-4! But note what the contrast is: 'He does not compare the righteous with the wicked; rather, he compares the object of the faith of the righteous – the nature of the LORD – with the beliefs and practices of the unbelievers.'[6] If we think in terms of evangelical hymnody, verses 5-9 are saying, Now ... 'turn your eyes upon Jesus.'

First off, David so much as says, Look how *refreshing* Yahweh's unchanging love is (vv. 5-6). He fairly ransacks the world describing the immensity of Yahweh's goodness in contrast to the dark smolderings of the wicked in the first segment. Yahweh's unchanging love (*ḥesed*) is in the heavens, His faithfulness reaches 'all the way up to the clouds'; His righteousness is 'like the highest mountains'. Literally, this last phrase is 'the mountains of God', but I take that, as it can be, as a superlative, the highest mountains. When he speaks of 'your righteousness', I take that primarily of God's right ways of acting toward and for His people. Then he plummets down from the highest mountains to the ocean depths – Yahweh's 'decisions' are 'a vast deep'. Probably David is not stressing the hidden mysteriousness of Yahweh's decisions or judgments but simply wanting to ring the changes on the reach and extent and vastness of Yahweh's justice and goodness.

6   Allen Ross, *A Commentary on the Psalms: Volume 1 (1-41)*, Kregel Exegetical Library (Grand Rapids: Kregel, 2011), 789.

He wants to stretch our faith to take in the infinite dimensions of Yahweh's unchanging love and goodness. That's the purpose of verses 5-6, beginning, as they do, with 'Yahweh' as the first word and ending with 'Yahweh' as the last word. And it is so delightfully refreshing – He has taken us out of the dark hole where the wicked is scheming (vv. 1-4) into the limitless spaces of unchanging love.

The change of mood here reminds me of an incident noted in *World* magazine a few years ago. Dorothy Fletcher of Liverpool, England, was on a plane headed for Florida. In flight she had a heart attack. Bad scenario – heart attack in a metal tube at 30,000 feet. However, when a flight attendant called for a doctor to tend the collapsed woman, within seconds fifteen cardiologists answered the call! They were en route to a conference on heart disease. She recovered and got to her daughter's wedding. Heart attack in flight – but with a plane-full of cardiologists. What could be better? That's the contrast verses 5-6 make in the face of verses 1-4.

But then in verses 7-9 David wants us to settle down and ponder Yahweh's unchanging love, especially how *rich* it is. Verse 7a is the keynote here – indeed, perhaps of the whole psalm: 'How precious is your unchanging love, O God!' It is precious because it is a *sheltering* love: 'the sons of man can take refuge in the shadow of your wings' (v. 7b). David specifies 'the sons of man'. He does not confine this benefit to Israel or the believers in Israel. It seems to be general – there is a kind of benevolent protection that humanity at large enjoys. And it is a *sustaining* love (v. 8). Here it looks (with the reference to 'your house') like Yahweh's own people are the beneficiaries. If verse 7 stresses Yahweh's protecting love, verse 8 underscores His providing love.[7] And all this is so because (note the 'For' in v. 9a) Yahweh Himself is so *sufficient*. Where there is a 'fountain' there is ongoing abundance and never any lack. One hesitates to nail down the figures too tightly, but verse 9 implies that Yahweh provides both our vitality ('the fountain of life') and our clarity ('in your light we see light'), the latter perhaps suggesting He provides all the direction we may need.

Let's back off and look at these five verses (vv. 5-9) as a whole and remember how they function in stark antithesis to verses 1-4. Verses 1-4 show us the wicked man in his darkness and depravity and deviousness – the perpetual bane of the saints. And then verses 5-9 explode with this vision of Yahweh's *ḥesed*. It is, to be sure, a turn-your-eyes-upon-Jesus-like moment. Fill your sight and your imagination with the splendor of Yahweh's *ḥesed* and the denizens of earth 'will grow strangely dim'.

Psalm 36:5-9 brings to mind an anecdote from Iain Murray's biography of Martyn Lloyd-Jones. In May 1980, within the last year of Lloyd-Jones' life, he was speaking at an East Midlands Church Officers' Conference. These meetings were in Shepshed where his friend Paul Cook was a pastor. Paul was undergoing a time of severe oppression of spirit and his wife Faith naturally shared a heavy load

---

7   Verse 8a may be a general figure or might refer to enjoying a sacrificial meal at Yahweh's sanctuary; the word 'wadi' in 8b refers to a seasonal streambed that is full with rushing water in the rainy season. Some think there is an allusion to Eden here since 'delights' is its plural form.

in this trial. So during an afternoon break Lloyd-Jones went to the manse to visit with Faith. He discussed Paul's condition with her; then, she said, at tea-time he went on for some five minutes in prayer for his friends. Faith Cook surmises that the best part of his visit was what occurred as the Doctor left. No one had to tell them that, given Lloyd-Jones' condition, they would not see one another again on earth. So he grasped her hand warmly and simply said, 'Remember the love of God.' Mrs. Cook's comment was, 'These words, perhaps more than any others, carried me through all the distress of the months that followed.'[8] Simple words, aren't they? But you can tell from the context they were neither trite nor flippant but poignant and moving. They capture the very thing David is saying beginning in verse 5: whatever the grimness and darkness you are facing ... *remember the love of God.*

Thirdly, we hear David's **petition** in verses 10-12. From his description of the wicked man in verses 1-4 and his confession of Yahweh's unchanging love in verses 5-9, he comes now to his specific plea in verses 10-12.

He is still held captive by Yahweh's unchanging love. His main petition is in verse 10 and begins with: 'Make your unchanging love go on and on for those who know you.' The verb means 'to draw out', that is, extend, continue, prolong, or, as I've put it, 'go on and on.' Verse 11 supplies the driving motive for this prayer, for there the shadow of verses 1-4 comes to the surface again; he needs protection from the 'foot of arrogance' and the 'hand of

---

8   Iain H. Murray, *David Martyn Lloyd-Jones: The Fight of Faith 1939-1981* (Edinburgh: Banner of Truth, 1990), 735-36.

the wicked'. Clearly, he is not in despair for he has his 'eschatology' (last things) straight – in verse 12 he sees the fall of the wicked, 'slammed down' and 'unable to rise'. But that (v. 12) is then, but verse 11 is now, and in these present circumstances Yahweh must interpose his *ḥesed*. When David prays, 'Make your unchanging love go on and on,' he means something like, 'Let it be activated,' 'Let it take effect, have traction' here in my need.

During the War between the States there was a huge difficulty over food – food for wounded and ill soldiers in the northern hospitals. They received the usual diet of fried meat, hard tack, and black coffee. That, of course, simply aggravated the diarrhea, dysentery, and other ailments that ravaged the men. Scurvy even put in its appearance – they needed fresh fruit and vegetables. It wasn't that the army couldn't get the right kind of food for its invalids. They had purchased vast quantities of it, and they had whole warehouses full of such goods. The trouble was that the army command was so incompetent that they could not get the food from warehouses to hospitals. No one was authorized to make the proper requisitions. Warehouses full of good food were within accessible distance to the hospitals but there was no man or set of men whose job it was to see that the food got to the hospitals. So men died.[9] The resources were there, but they were never 'activated'. That may be an analogy that helps explain David's petition in verse 10. As if he says, Don't let your *ḥesed* simply be what I admire and revel in (in vv. 5-9), but activate

---

9   Bruce Catton, *Glory Road* (New York: Doubleday, 1952), 108-109.

it, draw it out, keep bringing it into play, in my actual circumstances. 'Make your unchanging love go on and on' in the thick of where I have to live. Let it be my ongoing experience.

In Psalm 36 David is telling you that Yahweh's unchanging love changes everything. He wants you to get a clear and full view of it. He wants you to see how vast (vv. 5-6), how valuable (vv. 7-9), how vital (vv. 10-11), and how victorious (v. 12) it is.

Psalm 37

Of David.

(1) Don't let yourself get burned up over evildoers;
don't be envious of wrong-doers;

(2) for like grass they will soon wither
and like green growth they will fade away.

(3) Trust in Yahweh and do good;
dwell in the land and feed on (his) faithfulness.

(4) Find your delight in Yahweh
and let him give you the requests of your heart.

(5) Roll your circumstances upon Yahweh
and trust in him – and **he** will take care of it.

(6) And he shall bring forth your righteousness like the light
and your cause like noon-time.

(7) Be silent before Yahweh and wait for him;
don't get burned up over the one who makes
his way prosper,
over the man who carries out schemes.

(8) Let go of wrath and forsake rage;
don't get burned up – it only makes for evil;

(9)   for evildoers will be cut off,
        but those waiting for Yahweh – **they** will possess the land.

(10) And yet a little bit and the wicked will not be there,
        and you shall try to detect his place – but he's not there.

(11) But the humble will possess the land
        and find delight in the abundance of peace.

(12) The wicked keeps plotting against the righteous
        and gnashes his teeth over him.

(13) **The Lord** laughs at him,
        for he sees that his day is coming.

(14) Wicked men draw the sword
           and they pull back their bow
       to bring down the afflicted and needy,
           to slaughter those whose way is upright.

(15) Their sword will enter their own heart,
        and their bows will be broken.

(16) Better is the little the righteous has
        than the abundance of many wicked folks;

(17) for the arms of the wicked will be broken,
        but Yahweh keeps supporting the righteous.

(18) Yahweh knows the days of the whole-hearted
        and their inheritance will be forever.

(19) They will never be put to shame in a disastrous time
        and in the days of famine they will have enough.

(20) For the wicked will perish,
        and the enemies of Yahweh are like the glory
           of the pastures;
        they are finished off; in smoke they are finished off.

(21) The wicked borrows and does not pay back,
     but the righteous is gracious and giving;

(22) for those blessed by him will possess the land,
     but those cursed by him will be cut off.

(23) It's from Yahweh that the steps of a man
          have been settled
     and he delights over his way.

(24) When he falls, he will not be flattened,
     for Yahweh keeps supporting his hand.

(25) I have been young, yes, I have become old,
     but I have not seen the righteous forsaken
          nor his seed asking for bread.

(26) All day long he is gracious and lending
     – and his seed become a blessing.

(27) Turn from evil and do good
     – and dwell forever.

(28) For Yahweh loves doing justice,
     and he will never forsake his covenant ones;
     they are preserved forever,
     but the seed of the wicked is cut off.

(29) The righteous will possess the land
     and will dwell upon it forever.

(30) The mouth of the righteous utters wisdom
     and his tongue speaks what is right.

(31) The law of his God is in his heart;
     his steps will not slip.

(32) The wicked keeps watch on the righteous
     and seeks to put him to death.

(33) **Yahweh** will never abandon him into his hand
and will never condemn him when he is judged.

(34) Wait for Yahweh – and keep his way,
and he will lift you up to possess the land;
when the wicked are cut off, you will see it.

(35) I saw a wicked man, a ruthless man,
and flaunting himself like a luxuriant tree;

(36) then one passed by, and, why! – he wasn't there!
And I searched for him, but he was not to be found.

(37) Watch the whole-hearted,
and keep an eye on the upright,
for there's a future for the man of peace.

(38) But rebels will be exterminated together
– the future of the wicked shall be cut off.

(39) But the salvation of the righteous comes from Yahweh
– their safe place in time of trouble.

(40) So Yahweh has helped them and delivered them.
He will deliver them from the wicked and will save them,
for they have taken refuge in him.

Steady, Steady… 14

We can't ease into Psalm 37 with some nice little story because there are so many problems with Psalm 37 itself that demand comment. It's sort of like phoning up a home where your friends live and their toilet is blocked up, there's something burning on the stove, one kid has duct-taped the dog's snout shut, and someone is ringing the doorbell. Hence no one can talk to you just then, not until those matters are addressed.

So what 'troubles' does Psalm 37 bring us? First, there's no slick way of dividing up the psalm since it follows an alphabetical acrostic form (see Pss. 25 and 34). Each segment (usually every two verses) begins with the subsequent letter of the Hebrew alphabet. David then is working his way through his A-B-G's (well, he is Hebrew, after all) on the theme of the prosperity of the wicked. He doesn't set it out in nice, neat, distinguishable, overall divisions. It is, we could say, one psalm, indivisible, with instruction and insight for all. But difficult to 'organize' (at least for us western-like minds).

Secondly, the psalm has a sort of obsession with the 'wicked'. The term is used thirteen times (sometimes singular, sometimes plural); then there are synonymous terms in verses 1-2, 7, and 9. It's like friends who move into another home and find it infested with roaches: when you meet them, those roaches are all they can talk about. So here with the wicked. It's as if one can't get away from them. Obviously, believing experience is a *conflict*.

But then, thirdly, who are the 'wicked' anyway? I mean the wicked here in Psalm 37. Well, apparently, they are *Israelite* wicked. There's no particular reason to assume they are pagans. There are no Moabites floating around. So the wicked are those among the covenant people (card-carrying Israelites) who despise the faithful among the covenant people.

Then, finally, if the psalmist is dealing with the prosperity of the wicked, why doesn't he say far more that could be said about it? Obviously, he doesn't cover everything. Why isn't he more exhaustive? There are other texts like Psalms 49 and 73 and the book of Job that could add more. But we'd hate it if the Bible were written that way. Psalm 37 is an instructive meditation not a comprehensive essay (even though David does say all he wanted to say from A to Z, *à la* acrostic). You'd go into mental overload if a psalmist tried to be all-inclusive. He's not providing a total solution to every conceivable aspect of the problem but primarily directing God's people how to face the dilemma. A biblical writer can teach helpfully without doing so exhaustively.

Though it's difficult to divide Psalm 37 into hard and fast segments, we can trace a broad break-down.

First of all, we can say that David speaks of **your posture** (vv. 1-8). He puts his counsel in primarily negative form in verses 1-2 and 7-8, and in positive form in verses 3-6.

In the 'negative' counsel a lot has to do with attitude. Note the text:

> Don't let yourself get burned up over evildoers;
> don't be envious of wrong-doers... (v. 1)
>
> ... don't get burned up over the one who makes his way prosper,
> over the man who carries out schemes. (v. 7b)
>
> Let go of wrath and forsake rage;
> don't get burned up – it only makes for evil... (v. 8)

David is not saying you cannot observe or recognize or be concerned about the success of the wicked, but he is saying not to get sucked up into anger, rage, and envy over it. Don't become stressed, obsessed, and distressed over it. Three times David forbids us to get 'burned up', or to use a paraphrase, 'Don't get steamed up.'

Such a reaction is easy to come by. David himself demonstrated it when the tight-wad Nabal stiff-armed David's request for supplies in 1 Samuel 25; David was so ticked off he was ready to wipe out Nabal's whole household (1 Sam. 25:13, 21-22). We don't usually react with reflective rationality at such times – not even in situations of little importance. I recall an evening when my wife was hosting a women's Bible study in our home. I was out, but when I returned I divined what she had done. During the meeting she had gone into my study looking for a pen; she was in a hurry; she needed to make sure the pen worked, so she scratched a few trial swipes on a bit of paper on my desk. The problem was that the 'bit of paper' was one of about half a dozen bills I had paid, placed in envelopes, attached stamps, and had in a neat stack on my desk ready to mail the next day. And she had used the top one for a scratch pad and it looked like a four-year-old had scribbled all over it. Now when you see something like that, you don't calmly say to yourself: 'I see that my wife has woefully defaced this bill I had paid, which I am sure she did in the heat of the moment without careful thought, and I should probably go and speak to her about it.' No, you – or at least, I – erupt with something like, 'What on earth were you doing? Can't you tell a bill from scratch paper?' And so on. So David would say: 'No, don't go there; don't get your bowels in an uproar.' That's what he means when he says, 'Don't get burned up – it only makes for evil' (v. 8b).

David's positive counsel has mostly to do with action (vv. 3, 4, 5, and we can add 7a). Part of it advocates going on doing what we are supposed to be doing – 'Trust in Yahweh and do good; dwell in the land and feed on (his) faithfulness' (v. 3). You simply press on with what you are to do in faith and obedience. Someone asked Harry Truman what was the first thing he would do upon arriving home after leaving the White House. 'Take the suitcases up to the attic' was his reply. Just do the next thing that needs to be done. Nothing especially sensational. If we wonder how that trust (v. 3a) is expressed, verse 5 gives us a clue: 'Roll your circumstances upon Yahweh.' It is, literally, 'Roll your way,' or 'ways,' upon Yahweh, but I think by 'ways' he means circumstances, which must include any anger, perplexity, or distress you may have over the success of the wicked. The whole matter is left in Yahweh's hands; it is not fodder for any vigilante activity on our part.

Don't think that David is urging a stance of utter passivity. It's really quite 'activist'. Note:

> Trust in Yahweh and do good... (v. 3a)
> Find your delight in Yahweh... (v. 4a)
> Roll your circumstances upon Yahweh... (v. 5a)
> Be silent before Yahweh and wait for him... (v. 7a)

Even 'waiting for' Yahweh to act is an active affair. What David is pushing for is a posture of *non-idolatry,* that is, he wants to keep you from acting as if you are God, as if your effort will right the wrong, your rage correct the injustice. Don't begin to think that your seething, boiling anger will somehow produce equity. 'Leave to your God to order and provide.'[1] That is to be your posture.

Secondly, the psalm teaches you what **your perspective** should be (vv. 9-22). Note the 'For' at the first of verse 9; it supplies an additional reason for what David said in verse 8. He had said there 'forsake rage', 'don't get burned up' and then had attached a reason, 'it

---

1   From Katharina von Schlegel's hymn, 'Be Still, My Soul.'

only makes for evil.' Then follows verse 9, 'For evildoers will be cut off,' an additional reason for obeying his counsel. It also highlights the perspective, the viewpoint, God's people are to have, namely, to realize that the wicked are on their way out, 'in a little bit' they will be taken out of the way (vv. 9-11). David had already struck this note in verse 2.

That verb 'cut off' (kārat) is used in verse 9 and also in verse 22, at the beginning and end of this section I have perhaps arbitrarily blocked off. It also appears in verses 28, 34, and 38. But this 'cutting off' of evildoers really does seem to pick up the emphasis of verses 9-22. Note how David hammers in this idea. In verses 12-13, the scheming wicked is the object of the Lord's derision, for his ruin is definite – 'his day is coming' (v. 13b). In verses 14-15, the ruin of the wicked is ironically just; in fact, it will be self-inflicted (v. 15). Verses 16-17 assure that the power ('arms') of the wicked will be shattered (v. 17a), and verse 20 that whatever dominance the wicked enjoy is going to be transitory. If you get down that point of view, it will carry you through a lot of this trouble.

One's view of the future does largely determine present decisions and attitudes. There's a rather amusing story that Moffatt Burris (mentioned previously) of South Carolina has told. He was a captain serving as part of the 82nd Airborne in World War II. By 1945 German resistance was crumbling and American forces were pressing on but were at the moment stopped on the west bank of the Elbe. But Burriss was itchy over waiting around and so lured a couple of other soldiers to hop into a jeep with him and see what they could find. They drove for forty miles without seeing any signs of a German army. Then they rounded a curve and met a long line of German vehicles. The jeep stopped; the Germans stopped. A German captain asked Burriss what he wanted. He said, 'I'm here to accept your surrender.' The German was non-plussed. Behind him were hundreds of tanks and trucks and several thousand troops. In front of him were three men and a jeep. He suggested Burriss must be insane. Burriss replied, 'Not at all. I have a whole army of paratroopers and tanks behind me, and you have Russians right behind you. Do you want to surrender to me or to the Russians?' The upshot was that a deliberation took place, then the Lieutenant General went back over forty miles with Burriss in his jeep to regimental headquarters to arrange formalities of the surrender.[2] Several thousand troops surrender to three GIs? Yes, it was a matter of perspective. Burriss' argument was: Me or the Russians? It didn't take much calculation to think what surrender to the Russians might be like, given the swath of ruin, death, and destruction with which German armies (and thugs) had ravaged Russia's land and people. There would be no tender mercies there. That perspective, that viewpoint, determined things for them.

The same principle is at work in our text. David is saying you must take the long view; you must let 'last things' determine how you live in the present. Let what you know about the future destiny of the wicked control your disposition toward the difficulties, pressures, and conflicts of the present. 'For evildoers will be cut off'

---

2   T. Moffatt Burriss, *Strike and Hold* (Washington, DC: Potomac Books, 2000), 187-89.

(v. 9a), 'the wicked will perish' (v. 20a) – that's what keeps me from despair in the present age. Those 'waiting for Yahweh' (vv. 9 – and 34) can wait precisely because they know that their God has 'fixed a day in which he is going to judge the world in righteousness by a man he has appointed, having furnished assurance (of it) to everyone when he raised him from the dead' (Acts 17:31). That must be your perspective.

A third section highlights **your provisions** (vv. 23-33). Even before the wicked are finally taken out, while God's people are living in this topsy-turvy world where the wicked seem to thrive and succeed, even in the midst of such turmoil and troubles, they are hardly bereft of all comforts, for God supplies them in the thick of their troubles. Verses 16-17 have already hinted at this. What are these provisions – provisions, please note, that are in place not only when the pressure comes from the wicked as in our psalm, but in all kinds of distresses the saints face.

There is *providence* (vv. 23-24), by which God directs the believer's way from the first but also keeps him from 'going under' when overwhelmed:

It's from Yahweh that the steps of a man have been
settled,
and he delights over his way.
When he falls, he will not be flattened,
for Yahweh keeps supporting his hand.

The 'how' we may not grasp, but the fact that God's often unseen providence keeps His servants on their feet is indisputable.

This was part of Calvin's testimony. He had lost Idelette, his wife of nine short years. He wrote to his friend Farel: 'I do what I can to keep myself from being overwhelmed with grief.... May the Lord Jesus ... support me ... under this heavy affliction, which would certainly have overcome me, had not He, who raises up the prostrate, strengthens the weak, and refreshes the weary, stretched forth His hand from heaven to me.'[3] Legions of Christ's people could say the same – 'which would certainly have overcome me....' But it's a strange phenomenon: we may fall, but not headlong; we may be cast down, but not destroyed; we may be taken apart, but not taken away. There is this mysterious stability we have because Yahweh keeps supporting our hand (v. 24b).

Another provision is *sustenance* (vv. 25-26):

> I have been young, yes, I have become old,
> but I have not seen the righteous forsaken
> nor his seed asking for bread.
> All day long he is gracious and lending
> – and his seed become a blessing.

Some, I suppose, lampoon David's claim, implying that his field of observation must've been terribly selective. But note that David says he never saw the righteous *forsaken*, not that he's never seen him *afflicted* (Joseph Caryl). Note too that he puts it forth as a general observation of his experience and not as an iron-clad rule with no exceptions. But he is saying that in face of all his pressures

---

3   Thea B. Van Halsema, *This Was John Calvin* (Grand Rapids: Baker, 1981), 155.

the righteous is generally provided for (v. 25) and therefore he can be generous (v. 26).[4]

I think contemporary servants of Christ can sometimes be rather blind to such crass, physical provisions. In the middle of heavy trouble, do I still have daily bread? I may be in the pit of despair, but am I, in that despair, at my kitchen table staring down at a bowl of cereal? I may be going through deep anguish of spirit, but do I still enjoy reasonably good physical health? I may be at a loss in some dire turmoil, but do I still have a non-leaking roof over my head and a mattress underneath my restless body? Shouldn't I notice these gifts? Sometimes the weight of your troubles can cause you to lose sight of basic provisions that are staring you in the face.

Yahweh also provides *assurance* (vv. 27-29; and v. 33 as well). Look once more at verses 27-29:

> Turn from evil and do good
> – and dwell forever.
> For Yahweh loves doing justice,
> and he will never forsake his covenant ones;
> they are preserved forever,
> but the seed of the wicked is cut off.
> The righteous will possess the land,
> and will dwell upon it forever.

---

4 Verse 25 was 'the promise which Robert Baillie of Jerviswoode left to his young son George, when his estates were confiscated, and he was condemned to death at Edinburgh, December 24, 1684' (John Ker, *The Psalms in History and Biography* [1886; reprint ed., Birmingham, AL: Solid Ground, 2006], 67).

I hold that there is far more than meets the eye in these verses. Sometimes that's the case with things – they are far 'deeper' than you at first imagine. It was like that on opening day of the Baltimore Orioles baseball season in 1984. President Reagan was to throw out 'the first pitch'. There are presidents and other celebrities who are accorded this honor every year and a lot of sorry pitches are thrown. So Orioles' catcher Rick Dempsey greeted President Reagan and was telling him he could go just halfway between home plate and the pitcher's mound and simply lob his 'pitch' in from there. Reagan pretended to be listening to this counsel while he began ignoring it by backing up a few steps at a time all the way to the pitching mound. Dempsey got behind home plate. Reagan wound up and 'threw a dead strike, an aspirin tablet,' according to Michael Deaver. Deaver could hear the 'pop' in the catcher's mitt. Quite a surprise.

But there was more behind that than was obvious. Unknown to any but Reagan's own circle, he had spent the last six or seven weekends practicing his 'pitching' at Camp David. During break times Reagan would have a Secret Service man help him with his fastball. Which is why his throw to Dempsey on opening day came with a proper smack and splat.[5]

Now I think it's similar with verses 27-29. I suppose many expositors may see it as hyperbole; some don't even touch the claim of the text. But 'forever' occurs three times in these verses. I think that's significant. I think those 'forevers' must

---

5   Michael K. Deaver, *A Different Drummer* (New York: HarperCollins, 2001), 182-84.

be given full weight and that they must include life beyond death and imply resurrection.[6] Well, what sort of 'assurance' would it be if it only means something like: 'You will dwell on the land, that is, whenever the wicked are eliminated, you can possess it – until you yourself kick the bucket.' If it's only some sort of limited scope like that it makes a farce out of the assurance. And it stubbornly refuses to take account of the repeated 'forever'. We are talking about ultimates here; verse 28b clearly seems to have that tone: 'they are preserved forever.' And the only real consolation is if a word like verse 29 carries or includes a post-resurrection sense. Such a promise is not confined to a slice of time in this age but has to do with an everlasting possession in bodily resurrection on Yahweh's real estate. Some promises like these only make decent sense if you assume that they assume resurrection. This is surely a sure assurance.

You must, of course, decide if you will follow David's (and Yahweh's) directions. David leaves you with his counsel and sums it up for you in verse 34: 'Wait for Yahweh – and keep his way.' He appends primarily 'negative' considerations in verses 35-38 and 'positive' ones in verses 39-40. But 34a is his basic summary: Wait for Yahweh, and in the meantime as the wicked are running around loose remember that Yahweh is your 'safe place in time of trouble' (v. 39b).

---

6   P. C. Craigie (*Psalms 1-50*, Word Biblical Commentary [Waco: Word Books, 1983], 299) facilely dismisses any reference to or implication of life beyond death here. Many scholars break out in hives over suggestions of resurrection or eternal life in such texts. Others simply pass over the issue. You can check the commentaries on this part of Psalm 37 yourself and see.

Also by Dale Ralph Davis…

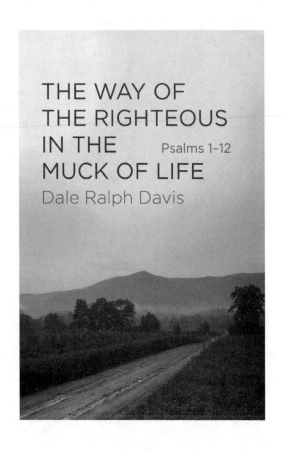

THE WAY OF
THE RIGHTEOUS
IN THE   Psalms 1–12
MUCK OF LIFE
Dale Ralph Davis

ISBN 978-1-7819-1861-6

The Way of the Righteous in the Muck of Life

Psalms 1–12

Dale Ralph Davis

In the opening pages of the Psalms, believers discover foundational truth for right living and great delight as children of God. Trusted theologian Dale Ralph Davis leads readers through a careful study of Psalms 1–12 with clear application for daily life.

As the first twelve Psalms continue, we see basic principles unfold with great clarity. Much like our troubles today, the Psalmist endured wickedness all around, a world hostile to the true God and on a very personal level deceit and persecution from his enemies. Readers are pointed toward the glorious rule of the Messiah, to whom the whole world belongs. In light of this realization, we are prepared to face all kinds of troubles that could cause despair. The righteous rely on God, and the Psalms teach us how. This book is ideal for use by small groups, as a teaching guide or for reference.

SLOGGING
ALONG IN THE
PATHS OF
RIGHTEOUSNESS

Psalms 13–24

Dale Ralph Davis

ISBN 978-1-7819-1304-8

Slogging Along in the Paths of Righteousness

Psalms 13-24

DALE RALPH DAVIS

Dale Ralph Davis plunges right into the middle of King David's hard times with a study that is resonant for our lives. King David's faith brought him through the muddy parts of life. Will we find that depression is our final response to a hard path? Will faith carry us across?

Find the encouragement that Psalms 13-24 hold for the Scripture-filled life.

Dale Ralph Davis has provided another faithful, lively and refreshing set of expositions. All Christians will benefit from this book and I hope it is read widely.

Sam Allberry
Apologist, Ravi Zacharias International Ministries;
Writer and Editor for The Gospel Coalition;
Author of *Is God Anti–Gay?*

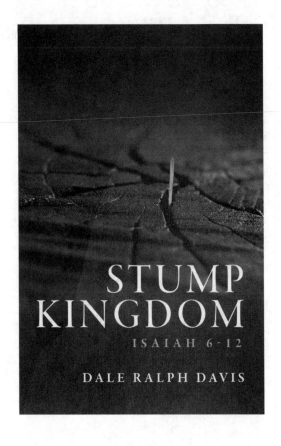

STUMP
KINGDOM

ISAIAH 6 - 12

DALE RALPH DAVIS

ISBN 978-1-5271-0006-0

Stump Kingdom
Isaiah 6-12

DALE RALPH DAVIS

Isaiah chapters 6-12 are overflowing with prediction, containing some of the most famous references in the Old Testament to the coming Messiah. Covering a time in Judah's history when it was being attacked and threatened on all sides, each chapter is full of rich biblical truths, revealing the character of Yahweh and His plan for His children. Although the remnant of His people would be reduced to a stump, a shoot would come forth – Immanuel, God with us.

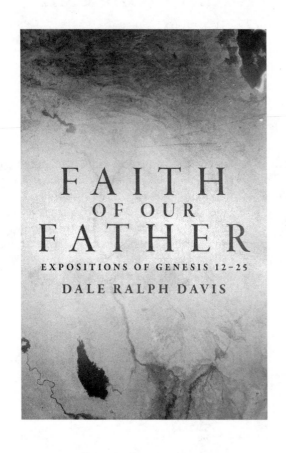

FAITH
OF OUR
FATHER

EXPOSITIONS OF GENESIS 12-25

DALE RALPH DAVIS

ISBN 978-1-7819-1644-5

Faith of Our Father

Expositions of Genesis 12-25

DALE RALPH DAVIS

With typical wit and wisdom Dale Ralph Davis opens up chapters 12-25 of Genesis. These beautiful and insightful expositions guide you through some of the early chapters of the Bible and will deepen your understanding of this important area of Scripture which help shape our understanding. This is an ideal resource for pastors as well small groups and personal study.

Ralph Davis is probably my favorite Old Testament expositor: he always unfolds the text with freshness, insight, and humor, leaving the reader with a clear understanding of what God is up to and the difference that should make in our lives. This volume on Abraham is a classic in the making!

Iain Duguid
Professor of Old Testament, Westminster Theological Seminary, Philadelphia, Pennsylvania

DALE RALPH DAVIS

THE WORD
BECAME FRESH

HOW TO PREACH FROM OLD TESTAMENT NARRATIVE TEXTS

ISBN 978-1-8455-0192-1

The Word Became Fresh

How to Preach from Old Testament Narrative Texts

Dale Ralph Davis

'...I still believe that traditional Old Testament criticism has had the effect of killing the Old Testament for the church. This little tome can hardly reverse that, but it is meant as an exercise in reading the Old Testament for fun and profit. As my mother-in-law used to say, "It's different anyway." And maybe it will help. Most of what I do in the following pages involves discussing examples of Old Testament narratives. I have tried to select examples from a broad range of possibilities. By the way, I assume that you have the biblical text handy in order to carry on your "Berean" work.' Dale Ralph Davis

There is no more gifted expositor of the Old Testament in our day than Ralph Davis. His book not only brings scholarly research to bear on the subject, but also reflects his many years of preaching week after week through the Old Testament. What a gift to the church to have such a fine book.

Richard Pratt,
President, Third Millennium Ministries, Orlando, Florida

Christian Focus Publications

Our mission statement –

STAYING FAITHFUL

In dependence upon God we seek to impact the world through literature faithful to His infallible Word, the Bible. Our aim is to ensure that the Lord Jesus Christ is presented as the only hope to obtain forgiveness of sin, live a useful life and look forward to heaven with Him.

Our Books are published in four imprints:

CHRISTIAN
FOCUS

popular works including biographies, commentaries, basic doctrine and Christian living.

CHRISTIAN
HERITAGE

books representing some of the best material from the rich heritage of the church.

MENTOR

books written at a level suitable for Bible College and seminary students, pastors, and other serious readers. The imprint includes commentaries, doctrinal studies, examination of current issues and church history.

CF4•K

children's books for quality Bible teaching and for all age groups: Sunday school curriculum, puzzle and activity books; personal and family devotional titles, biographies and inspirational stories—because you are never too young to know Jesus!

Christian Focus Publications Ltd,
Geanies House, Fearn, Ross-shire,
IV20 1TW, Scotland, United Kingdom.
www.christianfocus.com
blog.christianfocus.com